ATTENTION! THIS BOOK WILL MAKE YOU MONEY

ATTENTION! THIS BOOK WILL MAKE YOU MONEY

HOW TO USE ATTENTION-GETTING ONLINE
MARKETING TO INCREASE YOUR REVENUE

JIM F. KUKRAL

WILEY

John Wiley & Sons, Inc.

Published by John Wiley & Sons, Inc., Hoboken, New Jersey
Published simultaneously in Canada

For general information on our other products and services or for technical support, please
contact our Customer Care Department within the United States at (800) 762-2974, outside
the United States at (317) 572-3993 or fax (317) 572-4002.

Wiley also publishes its books in a variety of electronic formats. Some content that appears in
print may not be available in electronic books. For more information about Wiley products,
visit our web site at www.wiley.com.

ISBN 978-0-470-59927-3 (cloth)
ISBN 978-0-470-88066-1 (ebk)
ISBN 978-0-470-88067-8 (ebk)
ISBN 978-0-470-88068-5 (ebk)

Printed in the United States of America

10 9 8 7 6 5 4 3 2 1

Contents

Thank You   xi

Get My Attention!   xiii

Part I   1

1 Attention Marketing   3

2 No More Apologizing   7

3 Don't You Want to Be "That Guy!"?   8

4 How Do I Become "That Guy"?   13

5 Can My Business Be "That Guy!"?   18

6 From Idea to Success In Eight Hours   26

7 Press Releases Don't Get Press Anymore   30

8 Help Me Help You   35

9 Mark Cuban Hates Me 39

10 New Jersey Man Sells Brooklyn Bridge . . . for $14.95! 44

11 One Video Got My Message Through 46

12 The Million-Dollar Question! 49

13 26 Ways to Generate Killer Ideas 51

14 Three Truths to Coming up with Great Ideas 60

15 Do Think Outside of the Box and What Can Happen When You Do 62

16 Do You Market Outrageously? 65

17 You Can't Do It? That's the Wrong Way to Think! 70

18 What's Your Hook? 73

19 A Few More Things about Good Brand Names . . . 76

20 Determination, Diligence, and Discipline 81

21 Marketing and Sales 101 85

22 It's All about Pain 93

23 The Universal Truths of Selling on the Web 98

Part II 107

24 Making Money on the Web 109

25 Do People Really Make Millions Online? 111

26 So How Do People Make Money Online?   117

27 What's Your $$$ Number?   122

28 Membership Sites & Recurring Revenue, Oh My!   124

29 CD or DVD Continuity Programs   130

30 Boot Camps and Training Sessions   132

31 Group Coaching   134

32 Keeping Subscribers   136

33 Reusing Content   138

34 Bonuses Rule!   139

35 A Regular Guy Becomes the King of Continuity   140

36 The Tools   142

37 Got a Brand in Mind Yet?   144

38 Affiliate Marketing   145

39 Social Media   148

40 Can I Use Social Media to Make Money?   151

41 Need a Job, Try Facebook   157

42 More Power to the People (on Facebook)   161

43 Attention! Videos Can Make Money   165

44 Getting into the Online Video Game 176

45 Let's Get Viral! 180

46 Walking the Walk 188

47 How to Distribute Web Videos 192

Part III **195**

48 That Question Mark Guy 197

49 Speaking of Questions . . . 202

50 Farting Sounds Make Us Laugh,
But Is Anyone Buying? 205

51 Mmm, Mmm, Good! 208

52 Is All Attention Good? 214

53 Image Counts 217

54 Do You Have a Voice? 220

55 Crazy = Success Question 225

56 Why Do Some People Get Attention Yet
Can't Monetize It? 230

57 The Web Is Full of Copycats 234

58 Customer Evangelists Rule 237

59 Luxury versus Need 242

60 Getting Attention the Old-Fashioned Way   245

61 Power to the People   248

62 One "Hell" of an Attention-Getter   251

63 Astonish Me!   254

64 Does Making S#*% Up to Get Attention Work?   257

65 The Best Job in the World   259

66 Porn and Pancakes at Church   261

67 The Worst Is Sometimes Better Than the Best   263

68 Five Cents Is More Memorable Than Free   265

69 Sometimes It's the Little Ideas That Work Best   267

70 Stalker or Author? Who Cares? It Worked!   269

71 An Idea Turned into Millions!   271

Conclusion   This Book was Written for You   275

But Wait . . . There's More!   277

Index   279

Thank You

To my parents, Ken and Elaine, for their endless encouragement, support, and sacrifices that enabled me to achieve the success I have today. To my wife, Doreen, for believing in me and supporting me in this crazy adventure called entrepreneurism. This book is made possible because of you. Thank you.

Get My Attention!

Before we get started, I'd like to pose a challenge for you to consider while reading this book. It will be interesting to see if you take me up on it, and, of course, if you can do it!

Think of a unique way to get my attention. It has to be more than writing a blog post, Tweeting me, or anything simple like that. Find a way to get my attention beyond all the typical ways most people use. If you can do it, I'll send you a signed copy of this book (you can give this copy to a friend). I will also give you a private, no-cost one-on-one consulting session over the phone. But wait, there's more! If you can truly, truly impress me and get my attention, I'll also include a free prize!

You can do it. Use the stories and techniques in this book for inspiration. Be creative and good luck! All the information you need to get started can be found at AttentiontheBook.com.

—Jim Kukral

PART

I

1

Attention Marketing

ANYONE CAN GET attention, but not everyone knows how to make a pile o' cash or a ton of publicity from it. Case in point, you could dress up like a circus clown and walk around your office Monday morning in an attempt to get your boss to notice you, finally, and sure, everyone would notice you. However, you'd probably just be fired, and that's not the promotion you were looking for.

You may also try standing up in an airplane and yelling BOMB! while clutching your laptop. Yep, that would get *a lot* of attention from the airline attendant who had been ignoring you, but again, that's probably a one-way trip to a back room in some dungeon filled with FBI agents, when all you really wanted was some pretzels. Not a good plan either.

You can strip naked live on the Internet and expose yourself to the globe in hopes of getting the word out about your new consulting services. Sure, you'd probably get a lot of views, and possibly some wedding proposals, but would you get any business out of it?

The point is . . . it's easy to do something stupid to get attention. However, is that really the smartest way to go about being noticed? Absolutely not. You're not dumb, so trying to do something dumb to get what you want is, well, dumb!

The big questions that are going to be addressed in this book are: How do you get attention that helps you? And how do you use that attention to help you benefit in some way for your business or brand?

If you can master the art of successful Attention Marketing, you'll find an entire world of crème-filled, juicy goodness waiting for you.

- A world where you don't have to pay for advertising anymore.
- A world where everyone knows your brand.
- A world where people walk up to you on the street, shake your hand, and say, "You're that guy!"
- A world where you have any job or career you want.
- A world where you can leverage your fame into business deals and long-lasting relationships

How does all of that sound? But wait, there's more!

Getting attention isn't anything new. Since the dawn of time, successful people have learned how to harness the power of Attention Marketing for their own benefit. From billionaires to real-estate moguls to circus performers all the way to regular nonfamous people who just happen to be great at getting attention. So if they can do it, why can't you? The answer is that you can do it! You just have to be properly educated, inspired, and motivated to get it done. As the title of this book says: "This book will make you money!"

Have I got your attention yet? Keep reading.

This is important! Attention = Revenue! Here's a little secret. The original title of this book was Attention = Revenue! However, the publisher finessed it a bit. I guess they thought the new title would get more attention.

Attention does in fact equal revenue. It's absolutely true! If you can find ways to get attention for your business or brand, you can translate that into revenue one way or another, and darn it, I'm going to prove it to you in this book.

Please don't get caught up on the word "revenue" in terms of dollars only. Revenue can be defined as many different things. It can be things such as leads, or publicity, or even accomplishing a minor goal like getting the attention of one person in the world. The following is a list of some other things that can be considered revenue:

- Subscribers for your podcast or blog.
- E-mail signups.
- Being asked to speak as an expert at a conference.
- Being featured on television, radio, or someone else's web site or blog.
- A book deal with a major publisher.
- Leads for your sales team.
- Twitter followers and Facebook friends.
- YouTube channel subscriptions and video views.
- LinkedIn connections.
- Better career or higher paying job.
- Landing a new fancy client.
- Being quoted in the *New York Times* or the *Wall Street Journal*.

Remember, these can be many little things that can lead up to big things, so let's not assume we always have to hit the home run to measure success. We don't. In fact, it's more likely that the little hits will power you through to the winning run at the end of the game first.

So Who Are You?

You're probably a small business owner, blogger, entrepreneur, or executive who has had enough of books that don't really show you how to do things. Maybe you're in a job you love at a company that finally has to find a way to use the Web to generate success. Maybe you just want to find a way to pay for your kids' college education without having to slave at a job you hate for years with hardly any real pay.

It's time to get started on the path to success. *Attention!* will get you there.

2

No More Apologizing

First things first, if there's one thing we have to get into your head this very second it's that you have to stop apologizing for wanting to make money.

Someway, somehow, we have to get you to stop listening to the countless hoards of other experts, gurus, and social media purists who want you to believe that being successful online is all about "building community" and "having passion." Sure, those things are important, but let's be honest. At the end of the day, those are the means to get to the real goal; the real reason you are reading this book. The deep down dark secret that perhaps you don't want to admit to yourself or are afraid to admit in public is: **YOU WANT TO MAKE MONEY!**

Are you ready to get started? Let's go.

3

Don't You Want to Be "That Guy"?

SCOTT GINSBERG HAD an idea one day, "What if I put on a name tag and wore it all the time? I mean *all* the time, day and night. Would people respond to me differently? Would it change anything?" Little did Scott know at the time that it would change *everything* for him, and for the future legions of his fans who found inspiration and success from his example.

That day was monumental for Scott's life and career for two reasons. First, it was the day he created the attention getting idea (the easier part) and second, because it was the day he acted on it (the much harder part).

Let's start with the idea part. We'll cover the taking action part later on in this book.

Scott did it. He wore a name tag every day, 24-hours a day, no matter where he went or what he was doing.

Doing laundry on a Sunday afternoon? Name tag on. On a blind date your best friend set you up on? Name tag on. Riding a roller coaster at 115 miles per hour? Name tag on. Playing craps at 4 AM in Las Vegas? Name tag on. Taking your kids shopping at Target? Name tag on.

Think Scott is full of you know what? He couldn't possible wear that name tag all the time, could he? In fact, to show his commitment Scott got a tattoo of a name tag on his chest. Now that's conviction. Scott lives his brand, literally. His over the top commitment confirms to his tribe that he truly believes in what he says. This resonates with his audience and helps him build brand loyalty. Oh yeah, and it continues to help him get attention.

Did It Work?

Heck yeah it did. At the time of this writing, it had been 3,459 days of wearing a name tag. Scott has transformed from a hopeful college graduate with no early direction of what to do in life to being a widely sought after public speaker, author of multiple books, and master consultant to some of America's biggest firms and successful brands. He generates hundreds of thousands of dollars per year through the roles just mentioned. Not bad for a kid with an attention-getting idea fresh out of college, eh?

Emerging from the cocoon was no longer just Scott, but "Scott the Name Tag Guy." A brand metamorphosis of epic proportions! See more at www.hellomynameisscott.com.

Scott became a top example of "That Guy." You know that guy. It's the guy you see at a trade show and you say, "I love that guy!" People flock over to get a picture with him or to shake his hand and say thank you. It's the woman that always seems to have a big crowd of people surrounding her at all times. Maybe it's the guy who is constantly asked to appear on television as an expert or entertainer. The woman who radiates positivity and success and, therefore, everyone wants to be just like her. The guy you recognize on the other side of the street and you run through traffic to go and say hello to.

Oh yeah, "That Guy" is also the guy you give a lot of money to. You buy his books. You buy his consulting services. You click on his affiliate links and open his e-mails. You buy in completely, because you're now a fan, and secretly, you probably want to be him. As Seth Godin would describe, you're now part of his tribe, whether you like it or not.

So why wouldn't you want to be "That Guy"? There's definite power in it.

Being "That Guy" obviously has huge advantages. When you're "That Guy" you're always the center of attention. As we'll learn in this book, being the center of attention is a really good thing, if you know how to use it.

"That Guy" can do things you can't do. "That Guy" can get paid thousands of dollars to attend trade shows and speak to thousands of people. "That Guy" can get a 10-book deal from a publisher (which is unheard of but Gary Vaynerchuk did it). "That Guy" can attract thousands of people almost instantly to a live Ustream video broadcast. "That Guy" can use his massive lot of influence to bargain better business deals and partnerships and raise money for charity. "That Guy" has leverage.

Why? Because he's "That Guy." Curious about other people who qualify as "That Guy"? Here's a partial list (I couldn't list them all here). For a complete list (and to add or nominate your own candidate) please visit www.AttentiontheBook.com.

- Gary Vaynerchuk—Wine enthusiast and social media maven. Visit Garyvaynerchuk.com
- Chris Brogan—Social media's poster boy and community specialist. Visit Chrisbrogan.com
- Peter Shankman—Creator of Helpareporter.com and PR guru. Visit Shankman.com
- Billy Mays—The master of the pitch. (R.I.P.)
- Shawn Collins and Missy Ward—Affiliate Marketing's MVPs. Visit AffiliateSummit.com
- Matthew Lesko—The Question Mark Guy. Visit Lesko.com
- Joel Comm—Web entrepreneur and creator of the iFart application. Visit Joelcomm.com

- Darren Rowse—Professional blogger and Web publisher. Visit Problogger.com
- Susan Bratton—Digital Marketing Entrepreneur. Visit Personallifemedia.com
- Veronica Belmont—Tech and gaming-centric video host. Visit Veronicabelmont.com
- Julia Nunes—YouTube ukulele wunderkind. Visit Julianunes.com
- Mari Smith—Social media marketer and Facebook queen. Visit Marismith.com
- Tara Hunt—Influential tech entrepreneur. Visit Horsepigcow .com
- Loren Feldman—Actor, Comedian, and Web Provocateur. Visit 1938media.com
- Ted Murphy—Web entrepreneur and all around fun-loving guy. Visit Ted.me
- Lewis Howes—LinkedIn master marketer. Visit Lewishowes .com
- Jay Berkowitz—Master Web consultant and speaker. Visit 10GoldenRules.com

All of those people have "it," that thing that makes us (the audience) stand up, take notice of them, and then want to be them. They are able to get the attention of the rest of us because they do something better or more unique or more interesting than we do. However, their success isn't accidental and yours won't be either. The one thing that those people have in common that you need to have is that they are the best at what they do, yes, but then they go out and consistently do it repeatedly in a unique way that gets the rest of us to pay attention.

It's not good enough to be smart and know about your business. That's only step one in the process of becoming "That Guy." The next step is going out there and telling the world about it in a way that makes you get noticed before everyone else. That's the difference between being really good and being "That Guy." The good news is that you're already smart and you are already an expert at something. Now you only need to take the next step and find a clever, consistent way to get the word out.

If there is one thing people who get noticed have in common, it's that they all know how to produce tons of great content. There's simply no way around the fact that the Web is dominated by businesses and individuals who have something powerful to say and then find as many ways as possible to say it. Delivering the message is sometimes more important than the message itself. You know a lot about what you know a lot about. Find a way to deliver it to your audience in a way that will make them pay attention, and easily allow them to help spread the word.

Chris Brogan delivers his messages through his blog, Web videos, books, and countless speaking gigs. Shawn Collins and Missy Ward deliver their message though a trade-show event called the Affiliate Summit. Billy Mays was the master of pitching you a product live in-person or on television. Loren Feldman can get you to pay attention to him on Web video by saying things that the rest of us only think, but don't want to say.

How are you currently delivering your message to your audience? Is it through your blog? Great, but how about adding Web videos to that? Make your videos and upload them to YouTube, then post them on your blog. Now you've got your message delivered in two different places, all for the price of one. If you speak at events, are you recording the audio of your talk and then blogging about it later, or using it to give away as a bonus to your member program?

4

How Do I Become "That Guy"?

THE GREAT NEWS for you reading this book is that anyone can be "That Guy" And you don't have to be an Internet geek, a social media pundit, or any other online-related job function. The guy that works in the fashion industry can be "That Guy." The gal in human resources who's seen it all, heard it all, and has the stories to prove it can be "That Guy."

All it takes is understanding the basic principles of how to get attention, then a solid plan (and a lot of hustle) to put yourself or your business out there so that customers know who you are.

Let's take Gary Vaynerchuk, for example. As a Russian-born immigrant, he turned his father's small liquor store into a $50 million business all before he was old enough to drink legally. However, he wasn't done yet. Gary then proceeded to build a mega personal brand for himself all by using social media and a lot of hustle. Gary became "That Guy" easily in comparison to the traditional path we all used to have to follow. Okay, it was a lot of hustle and hard work, but "easy" in terms of not having to spend millions of dollars in advertising to get there.

How did Gary do it? Social equity > financial equity. Those are Gary's words, not mine. The significance behind social equity > financial equity is that it's way more valuable these days to have a million friends or followers on social media outlets like Twitter and Facebook than it is to have a million dollars in advertising to spend. Why? Because the world is changing. We're much more connected than we have ever been before. Social media enables us to share every detail of what we're doing with anyone who's interested in hearing the answer to that question. Having one million people in your social equity circle means you have an unlimited group of rabid fans who are more than willing to spread the word about you or your business.

Gary's theory isn't unproven either. He's the perfect case study on how to reach his carefully and brilliantly constructed hypothesis. Just look at how he built himself into a top-selling author and professional speaker, all on the backs of the groups of fans who continue to grow in his social circles. That's why it's so important to be everywhere nowadays. Many people don't want to get on Facebook or try Twitter because they think it's a waste of their time.

The question is how is it a waste of time to build a network of resources or contacts? That's what we're doing here. It's not about getting more friends. C'mon, nobody wants a million friends. What we want is a network of people we can tap into when needed. A group of fans that can help us do things like research, find a new job, refer a product or service, or pass our information on to someone that could use it.

Joe the Banker versus Sue the Banker

Are you not sure that you need to use social media? Here's a story about Joe and Sue that might hit home for you.

Joe and Sue are both bankers who were laid off on the same day from the same company. Times are tough and the banking industry isn't as profitable as it used to be. Jobs are now scarce and hundreds of thousands of previously employed people are without jobs to provide for their family. When Joe and Sue found out that they had lost their jobs, they each took a different path to finding a new job. Joe is one of those people who never bought into the whole social media hype. "Why do I need more friends?" he said. "It's a waste of my time." Sue, however, realized long ago the power of networking online. She's amassed hundreds of Twitter followers, and has just as many Facebook friends and LinkedIn connections. In addition, there is her blog where she has a complete resume of her skills and full contact information.

The first day after Joe loses his job, he heads out to grab the morning newspaper and begins to scan the classifieds. He also calls a few friends who might know of something, and he even calls a professional recruiter. Then he goes online to look for openings. His job search has begun. Sue, on the other hand, started the job search minutes after she was laid off. She immediately told all of her followers about it on Twitter, possibly using her smart phone to update her status. Minutes after that, she updated her profile on LinkedIn and notified every contact there that she was available and looking for work. Then she updated her Facebook status and wrote a blog entry about her experience along with what kind of work she was looking for.

So who got the job quicker? Of course, it was Sue. The power of social media enabled her to send her message out to more people much faster than Joe could. Her associations with friends also enabled her to be recommended personally by someone who might have a connection inside a company she is hoping to work for. Joe, on the other hand, is still checking the classified ads. Do you want to be Joe or Sue?

Social Media Brand Explosion

I've been promoting the Jim Kukral brand online for close to 15 years now. In 2001, I bought the domain name JimKukral.com and began to blog about every day things, such as being cut-off on the road on the way to work or how the tragedy of 9/11 changed my life, and yours. My first blog wasn't about business. Heck, nobody back then was using blogs for their businesses. It was all about building your brand by letting people around the world, people normally outside of your circle of influence, come in and learn more about you. It was years later that I began to utilize blogs as a marketing and business tool, way before anyone else (blatant brag).

I wrote one of the first eBooks online that explained how to make money from a blog. The year was 2003 and it was called *Blogs to Riches*. The eBook contained tips and strategies for how to use your blog to build a personal brand and then how to turn that brand into revenue. Actually, you could say *Blogs to Riches* was a precursor for this book in many ways. When I first launched the eBook, I received tons of publicity from it, unfortunately 90 percent of it bad. I was getting hate mail from people saying things such as, "Blogging is pure, you can't make money from it you jerk!" or "You're an idiot. Nobody will ever make any money from a blog." Indeed, the same types of things people were saying about social media in the beginning.

I continued to blog for years and years, accumulating thousands of search engine rankings from articles that I had written. I spent a year creating a new Web video every single day, getting my message out to an entirely new audience. I created podcasts of interviews with experts and gurus. I built my brand over those years to a place where I was quite well known in my industry circles, and it worked great. I had a loyal following of people subscribed to my RSS feed and e-mail newsletters; in addition, I had earned myself a very nice reputation as someone who knew how to help other people find success online.

However, it wasn't until social media really came along that my brand exploded. Because of social media, I was able to extend my brand and expand my reach, allowing me to generate thousands upon thousands of direct contacts who were interested in me and what I do. Here's the key point: These contacts were people outside of my regular inside circle. You know, customers. You can't pay for that kind of attention, and that's one of the best things about using social media to build your brand. It's free!

Lewis Howes was able to launch a career as a sports management consultant, highly paid speaker, and top Internet marketer by using social media the right way in very little time. Two years earlier, nobody knew who Lewis was, yet because of his ability to get out there and put in the time and effort needed to build his social circle, he has been able to do what would probably have taken him a million dollars and 10 years to do before.

Winelibrary TV creator, Gary Vaynerchuk has gone from a virtual unknown to a highly paid keynote speaker and consultant, best-selling author, and voice of an entire industry. Between the years 2007–2009, it was almost impossible to not see Gary featured somewhere online or even in the traditional media. Television shows like Ellen, Conan O' Brian, and more understood that Gary brought with him more than knowing a crap-load about wine. They realized that Gary brought an audience with him.

"That Guy" can bring a ready-made audience with him at a moment's notice. In today's crowded and noisy marketplace, "That Guy" is someone everyone wants to know, and certainly, somebody everyone wants to tell the world that they know.

5

Can My Business Be "That Guy"?

REMEMBER, YOU DON'T have to be an individual person active online to be "That Guy." Your business can be "That Guy." Just think about the businesses that always seem to be at the top of everyone's list, constantly being mentioned, and featured in the media and covered by blogs. Those businesses have tapped into something unique, and are able to get you and me to flock to them, not only making us fans of what they do, but how they do it. For example, take Zappos. Sure, they're one of the biggest online retailers on the planet, but what really gets them noticed is their amazing customer service. Zappos teaches us valuable lessons that we can take and implement in our businesses, which makes them more than just a place for us to buy shoes.

Below are some other businesses that qualify as "That Guy."

Apple

No longer the choice for just the artsy types and Mac fan boys, Apple is adored by investors, consumers, and legions of others who have a cult-like worship for CEO Steve Jobs and his Zen philosophy of sleek design and function. Jobs's return to the company he founded was heralded and led to the release of Apple's iTunes and iPod, which revolutionized how music is bought and listened to. The company's iPhone, iPad, and apps marketplace also paved the way for a new generation of smart phones and portable computing devices. In addition, the company continues its tradition of innovative advertising. Therefore, even if you consider yourself a PC person, you can't deny Apple's marketing muscle and mass coolness appeal.

Twitter

Letting your followers know your thoughts in 140 characters has become a major obsession for everyone from celebrities to CEOs to big businesses to moms around the world. Twitter's tens of millions of users value the ability to interact with their community of followers in real-time and see what others are saying. Often news events are reported first on Twitter, beating the mainstream press to the punch. The real-time search allows marketers and businesses to see what people are interested in, saying about them, and monitor their brands. Twitter also spawned numerous other apps around it and helped business reach out more effectively to embrace and engage customers. The businesses that have leveraged Twitter successfully have gained respect from customers, improved their service, garnered brand recognition, and ultimately improved their bottom line.

Mashable

Mashable is fast becoming the online bible of the social media set. It's a daily must read for anyone engrossed in social media, using social media as part of their business strategy, or just a social media fan. Its combination of timely news, analysis, and humor has won over readers and siphoned an audience from venerable tech blogs.

Virgin America

Let's face it, flying has become somewhat of a hassle. But Sir Richard Branson has brought style, service, and the customers' comfort back to the skies. Instead of feeling like herded cattle, passengers are treated like first-class passengers—even while in coach. Launched in 2007, Virgin American offers travelers a very sexy, chic, European feel, in-flight Wi-Fi, touch screen entertainment in each seat back, a cheery interior, and very competitive pricing. Virgin America quickly became the darling of the travel industry and a new favorite of frequent fliers.

Jet Blue

It's like flying but from your living room recliner. Jet Blue was the first airline to offer satellite TV from your seat back—letting you watch that Law & Order marathon on TNT from Los Angeles to New York. Jet Blue's routes to mainly metropolitan cities coast-to-coast make it perfect for taking cross-country red eye flights. Discount fares and a playful attitude have won the hearts of travelers. Its outreach to customers via Twitter and Facebook fan pages has given the company a fun way to interact with customers, offer special fares, and improve its service. Jet Blue has also been among the few airlines that has not implemented baggage fees, still offers snacks, and provides free Wi-Fi to travelers.

Blogher

Taking girl power to a completely new level, Blogher was the first network to offer women bloggers the ability to be heard like never before. Beginning with the Blogher conference in February 2005, the company was the brainchild of founders Lisa Stone, Elisa Camahort Page, and Jory Des Jardins. The network followed and gave women bloggers a way to make money for creating their valuable content. The company's targeted vision to promote, encourage, and uplift women has made it a powerhouse for brands looking to connect with women bloggers and has already taught the guys a thing or two.

Craigslist

Need a used car, a salad spinner, a date, a new apartment, a hamster, a job, or tickets to a sold out concert? You can find it all on Craigslist. It's the place to find nearly everything you need for your life. The free service started as a list of events in San Francisco in 1995 and quickly spread to nearly every major city in the United States. Craigslist's appeal is that is has remained free and doesn't accept advertising. Only those posting jobs pay for listings. In addition, Craig Newmark, the company's self-proclaimed nerdy founder has remained on board personally dealing with customer service on a daily basis, giving the service a much more personal feel. It's also community moderated, which contributes to each region's version of Craigslist having a homey feeling reflective of that community. Fun additions to the service like "the best of Craigslist" where odd, funny, and downright weird posts are highlighted, help make it a daily destination for millions.

Turkey in a Bottle

Did you ever think you might want to drink soda that tastes like turkey and gravy, green bean casserole, or mashed potato and butter? Mmmmmm, not quite, right? However, that kind of soda really does exist, and its creator, Jones Soda out of Seattle, was able to leverage the massive attention they received from the creation and promotion of those flavors into sales and publicity, in a *big* way.

The market for beverages is a billion-dollar business. Every year, thousands of new libations make their way into the marketplace vying for consumer's attention, and consumption (burp). The problem is that, as in any competitive business space, only a few will survive. There's simply too much competition out there for all of them to make their way into your refrigerator then down your throat into your belly. The team at Jones already had a great product and brand, but like most companies, they needed something to help put them over the edge. Something that would get the attention of not only the consumers out there who buy their soda, but also the buyers at the large grocery chains around the country who stocked their shelves with things their customer's crave.

I interviewed former Founder and CEO of Jones Soda, Peter Van Stolk, to find out more about Jones's success:

Jim: So how did the idea for the unorthodox soda flavors come to pass?

Peter: We wanted to grow the business like everyone else, so we kept asking ourselves the same question: How can we capture attention when our competitors have a billion marketing dollars to spend? It's a challenge for sure. We decided to think differently and instead play by our rules, not theirs. Traditional marketing is setup by the rules of the greatest spender, so we decided to capture attention another way. In the food industry, you have slotting fees where you pay for shelf space. So it's really about how much you have to spend, not about how good your product is.

We needed to make a splash and get our brand out there by appealing to the press to do it for us. In the soft drink business, the competitive spending is typically in the third quarter of the year, or roughly from Mother's Day to Labor Day. So it's very hard to get free press in that time period because the media sells a lot of ads during that time. We decided to try to get media attention after Labor Day instead. We looked at Thanksgiving, which was mostly void of marketing in the soda business.

I was driving in my car one day when I had the idea that would change things for us. I immediately called my VP of Operations and told him I wanted him to make a

Thanksgiving themed soda—something with turkey—and I wanted to give all the proceeds from the sale of that soda to charity.

Jim: What did people say to you when you told them your idea?

Peter: I was the boss, and Jones was full of fun, creative people, so nobody told me it was a bad idea. They all just said, "Let's do it." And we did. Our roots had always been about having fun so this wasn't any different. We'd been doing crazy things for years before this. I used to get my guys to change the color of their hair to match the soda, or dress in orange jumps suits, or put flames on trucks to promote the brand. We would look for places that were not typical places you'd put soda into. Places like skateboard shops, tattoo shops, and even sex shops. People didn't understand what we were doing, but we had to do these kinds of things. We were competing against giants.

Jim: What were the results?

Peter: We launched the campaign before Thanksgiving and we were giving all the proceeds to Toys for Tots. The response from the media and consumers was unbelievable. I think we received about $8 million in press the first year and we quickly sold out of the inventory we had made. So for our second year we made more flavors and more inventory. The demand was so great that year it crashed our server. It worked so well we sent out a press release after saying we had 100 percent market share on the meat flavored beverage category. People were beginning to notice me in the grocery store and other places coming up to me and saying, "You're the guy with the turkey soda! I can't get any, you sold out!"

Overall, over the years, we estimate we saved $15 to $25 million in marketing costs. The company grew from $22 million to $40 million in that 4-year span.

So let's get this straight in case you missed it. Pete had a fun, crazy, potentially attention-getting idea while driving in his car one day. He put it into action, his business received $25 million in free marketing, and his business grew from $22 million to

$40 million. How many ideas have you come up with while driving that you've written off? When you're working out and you come up with a fresh idea that makes you laugh, do you go out and try it, or do you blow it off and say it will never work? Jones Soda is proof positive that perhaps those ideas you've been throwing in the trash can are worth millions.

People like Peter know that you have to stop being afraid of trying new things if you want to find success. "What's the worst that can happen?" said Peter. "I started with nothing, and worked my ass off to build my business up with some fun ideas. If you're afraid to try, then you're afraid to win, and if you continue down the same path without results, you can't win. Motivation for change is based on fear. If you're afraid to make a mistake that means you're living in a fantasy world, not everything is going to work. It's crazy to be afraid to make a mistake."

Of course, the Jones Soda brand could not have been so successful without its fans leading the way. "Look, without evangelists, without fans, we're just another soda company. We changed the game. We made soda a treat, not a food. Our fans followed the media coverage and took it to the next level of word of mouth, one that we couldn't even begin to measure."

So why don't we see more businesses trying to copy the Jones Soda model of coming up with unique, fun, or crazy ideas? Why can't you do it? If you're part of a big company, you may not be built to be the trendsetter. You focus on what's selling and leave the trend spotting to people like Jones Soda. However, if you're a small business owner competing with giants in your industry, what do you have to lose?

Is what Jones Soda did really such an outrageous idea? If you own a restaurant, you could develop your own outrageous culinary concoctions to get people talking about you. Imagine you had a broccoli and chocolate soufflé on your menu, and imagine it was actually good (I know that's difficult). Now imagine the reactions you'd get from customers every time you pulled out the dessert cart and menu. The customers who were brave enough to order it would be amazed at how good it was, and guess what they're going to do after they eat it? They're going to tell the world about it on Twitter, Facebook, in their next business meeting, on their blog, to their neighbor, and so on. Even the customers who didn't take the risk to try it are going to remember it, and they're going to spread the word just like everyone else. Pretty soon, you're finding people coming to your restaurant just to try it based on a recommendation they received from a friend. This is word of mouth at its finest, using attention to make it happen. On the other hand, maybe you'd rather just keep spending thousands of dollars on advertising instead of trying to be creative. It's up to you.

Jones Soda also offers another unique product to its growing customer base, so don't forget to try out the MyJones.com custom branding. There, customers can get their own custom-designed bottles of Jones Soda designed for themselves or a friend. You can have a few cases made up with your bio and link to your resume on the label, and then send them out to prospective employers. Alternatively, print some up with your sales message and send them out to prospective clients. It's a sure-fire way to get attention.

6

From Idea to Success in Eight Hours

THERE I WAS, watching myself on the six o'clock news being interviewed in the kitchen of my home. Little did I know that 8-hours earlier I would have come up with a spur of the moment idea that would get me there.

Having been born and raised in Cleveland, Ohio, I am, of course, a die-hard fan of the Cleveland Browns football team (pity me). It was Christmastime in the year 2006 and the Browns were at the end of yet another disappointing season of more losses than wins. I and every other fan were frustrated beyond belief after another losing season. To make matters worse, the next Browns game was scheduled on Christmas Eve and weather forecasts were calling for freezing temperatures and blizzard-like conditions.

Now typically Browns fans don't have a problem selling out the stadium, yet because of the timing and weather, there was a growing rumble in the air that fans weren't going to show up. Who wants to freeze their butts off on Christmas Eve rooting for a losing team when they could be at home instead spending time with their families, waiting for Santa and hitting the eggnog? In the NFL, when you don't sell all the tickets for a game, the game is blacked-out on television locally, and since this hadn't happened in so many years, the local media was hot on the story.

Tip: Keep your eye out for hot topics and trends. The media is constantly looking for timely stories. With some skill and practice, you can usually weave your product or service into a trending topic/story.

I arrived at my office the Tuesday before the game and had a spur of the moment idea: I wondered if I could get on the news by creating a media story out of nothing. Ah, a challenge! The first thing I did was go and see if the domain name FanProtest.com was available. It was! Seven dollars and ninety-five cents later, using Godaddy.com, I was ready to build a web site with a message that I knew would get attention. The concept was this: We, the fans, have had enough with the team being bad, so we're going to protest this Christmas Eve game by not showing up or buying the remaining tickets. That'll show the owner of the team we mean business, right?

Of course, it really wouldn't, I realized that. However, I was pretty sure I could get the media to bite on the story. The first thing I did was create a simple web site with that simple message. Then I created a short video of myself talking about the protest. The video was uploaded to YouTube and then placed on my web site. The whole endeavor took me about 45 minutes, at best. The next part was crucial: I always maintain an updated list of local and global press contacts in an Excel spreadsheet. I sent an e-mail out to all the pressroom contacts at every local television and radio station, including the Associated Press (AP). See the e-mail I sent on the following page.

That was it, short and sweet. I sent that e-mail to about ten local press contacts, went back to work, and waited to see if anything would happen. A few hours later, I headed home for the day, and when I walked in the door, my wife handed me the

Subject line: New Movement: Protest the Browns!

We, Browns fans, are fed up. The team stinks again this year, and now we're expected to come to a game on Christmas Eve and pay for parking, food, hats, and drinks? Enough! The owner of the Browns, Mr. Lerner, needs to see how serious we are. That's why we're working to protest the game.

Watch the video here at www.fanprotest.com.

For more information, contact Jim by replying to this e-mail.

Sincerely,

Jim Kukral

FanProtest.com

phone and said, "Someone is on the phone for you from Channel 3 (WKYC) news and they want to talk to you about your fan protest thing." Surprised, I picked up the phone and found myself talking to a producer who wanted to interview me on camera about the story for that night's news broadcast. Success!

An hour and a half later, I had a camera crew and reporter in my kitchen doing a story on me and my last minute, half-cocked idea. The 2-minute piece ran that evening on the news, about 8 hours or so after I came up with the idea. Not too shabby I must say. After the piece ran, my phone started ringing off the hook from friends, family, and clients who were either laughing hysterically or complimenting me, or both.

Now, I'm fully aware that I must have caught the news department on a so-called "slow news day," but who cares? I was able to create an attention-getting idea in less than an hour for less than 10 bucks that got my brand on the news in less than 8 hours. That's a win by any public relation firm's standard for sure. It's proof positive that anyone can get attention, even a small amount, with a creative idea and some very basic implementation and costs.

Perhaps the best part of the story is that because of the publicity I received from the story, I was able to connect with several brand-new potential clients who had never heard of me. They saw the story and followed the link to my main web site and learned that I was a small business Web consultant, then contacted me and eventually hired me. This work accounted for thousands and thousands of dollars of income for me over the next few months, all from about an hour of work on my part. Not a bad return on investment (ROI), eh?

There's an opportunity for you to get your business or brand in the news in a similar fashion, assuming you can capitalize on trending topics or news stories.

7

Press Releases Don't Get Press Anymore

IN THE DAYS before the Internet and social media, press releases did get press, but times have changed. We used to be able to generate a press release about our "ground-breaking" product or service and send it out over the news wire and get it in front of media gatekeepers, who would then decide if it was newsworthy or not. This outdated system became obsolete quickly in the first part of the twenty-first century.

To get the media to pay attention to you now, you have to step up your game and get them to look your way using strategies bigger than a simple press release. That's good news for you and me, as it opens up the door for us to more easily reach these influencers and get our message out. However, the problem is that journalists, television and radio producers, and editors are also now bombarded with more messages than ever and they now have the ability to use Internet search engines and social media to more easily do their research.

The following are a few ways you can get the attention of the media to achieve fantastic results for you and your business.

Use a Rifle, Not a Shotgun

I really dislike the word blast. In the Internet world, the word blast has been used for years to describe things like mass e-mails of press releases sent to distribution lists. We were told to "blast out an update to our subscribers," or "blast out a news release." Ugh. Who wants to be blasted to or at? Nobody. Who are we? Dick Cheney? Besides, the approach doesn't work as it used to— especially in the news release category. The best way to get attention from someone in the media today is to go one-on-one.

Identify key members of the press and build yourself a database of those contacts. It's pretty easy to build your initial list. Simply browse the Web and search for the contact information for each media outlet. Each will probably have a different way they'd like to be contacted, although most will offer you a generic e-mail address for sending in news stories, tips, or other inquiries. This is true for places like magazines, blogs, television or radio stations, newspapers, or just web sites. Public relations firms, or any worth their salt, will already own such a list, which is more than likely very large and covers specialized and general interest outlets, which is part of what they charge you for.

Public relations (PR) firms will also have the second thing you will need: personal connections. David Pogue writes the technology column for the *New York Times*. He has stated publicly that he gets more than 1,000 pitches a day. Yes, 1,000 pitches a day! With that many pitches, how are you possibly going to get through to him? The odds are not in your favor. However, if you have an existing relationship with Mr. Pogue, you're probably standing a better chance of him paying attention to you.

Remember, members of the media have a job to do. They're like Google. Google has to solve problems for their customers, the Internet searcher. If they can't do that, they lose customers. The same goes for a member of the media. Their job is to get more viewers, readers, listeners, and so on. Therefore, they need good stories to feature. You can become a valuable resource for them.

Someone they can count on to deliver high quality, relevant information that helps them beat their deadline. You can be their Google. Consider treating your media contacts like your customers. Learn about what they need and deliver *only* that to them in the way that they want it. Off-topic pitches are a waste of time and will quickly push you into the spam folder.

The Pitch

Here's what has brought me much success. The first thing I do when I want to introduce a story idea to someone in the media is call them up. However, don't just call them and start pitching. Instead, when you call them, follow this script:

Reporter: Hello, this is Mary in *Lifestyle*.
Me: Hi Mary, my name is Jim Kukral. I have an idea for a story I'd like to give you. Do you have 1 minute right now? If not, I can call you back. I understand you may be on deadline.

Journalists love this because it's true. They are probably on deadline, and you're interrupting them. If you're conscious about their time, they will usually respect you more and listen to you. Now, if they say they have time right then, then you need to have your pitch ready! You should practice this ahead of time, and it should be about 30-seconds long, that's it. Of course, it should be pertinent to them or you're really wasting their time, which will get you nowhere. Make sure you have the right person on the phone. Here's a sample pitch that will get you noticed:

Me: Great, thanks. Did you know that the United States Department of Education has recently reported that overall online learning environments actually lead to higher test performance than face-to-face learning environments? The *New York Times* reported this. I have a link to the story and document I will send you. Now, I read your article last week where you talked with teachers who are giving out homework online. There's now a piece of Web software that takes that even further. It's called Prfessor.com, and it allows anyone, regardless of tech skills, to create their very own online university, academy, or training center instantly. Moreover, the best part is, those same teachers or school systems can use it to generate profits for themselves or for their school districts, helping to supplement long-lost budgets and cutbacks. Do you think I could send you some more information via e-mail about this?

That's it. The reporter is either going to buy the pitch or say no thanks. Chances are, though, that if you hit them with a good pitch with all the right elements in place you're going to have a much better chance at getting them interested in what you have to say. Let's dissect the pitch and pull out the main parts that make it so good.

- Lead with credibility—Statistics are always a great way to lead in. This gives the reporter something to legitimize the story with. It shows you've done your research and legitimizes your pitch.
- Do some research—Notice how I referenced an article of theirs? That shows that I'm not just pitching blind. It shows that I have spent the time to understand what they are looking for and I'm not wasting their time.
- The pitch—Now I introduce the product and give solutions to the problems that the product solves.
- The benefit—Your pitch should always show them what potential benefits can come from using the product.
- The call to action—Always leave them with the next steps. In this case, I asked the reporter if I could follow up with them via e-mail. If they say yes, I send over a short note thanking them for their time, including a short summary of the pitch and the information I promised I'd send them, and include my name and full contact information.

Don't be discouraged if your pitch doesn't make it through either. The reporter may have decided not to use your idea this time, but could in the future. Ensure you follow up with them a week or so afterward (just once).

Megan Megale's 12-year-old daughter, Shea Megale, suffers from a disease called spinal muscular atrophy. Shea had produced a book series and was hoping to get the word out about it in a big way, specifically trying to get the attention of a reporter at *USA Today*. Therefore, mom, Megan, decided to take her skills as a public relations professional and try something a bit different. Instead of doing the usual e-mail or phone call strategy, Megan bought a Carvel ice cream cake and wrote her phone number and the words "call me" on it and dropped it off personally at the reporter's office. Five minutes later Megan got a call from the reporter. Long story short, the story ran in the paper, which led to Shea getting booked on the *Today Show* and the *Evening News with Katie Couric*.

8

Help Me Help You

Peter Shankman, author of *Can We Do That? Outrageous PR Stunts That Work—And Why Your Company Needs Them*, has spent a career in public relations helping both publicity seekers and media help each other. Once a year, Mr. Shankman sends out an e-mail to his list of media contacts offering his assistance. No, not trying to get publicity for him or his clients, but rather simply offering up his Rolodex. The concept is, "I'm a well-connected businessman. I can help you get sources for stories, or introduce you to people who can help you accomplish *your* goal of putting out content and meeting your deadline. Contact me anytime."

Talk about building relationships. Does it work? Oh yeah. This approach helps endear Mr. Shankman to his media contacts, which then, of course, helps him get attention for himself and his clients. Probably the biggest thing that came out of this clever idea was a project called Help a Reporter Out, or HARO (www.helpareporter.com).

HARO is the natural extension of Mr. Shankman's yearly e-mail to his media contacts. HARO takes the concept of helping to another level; it enables anyone looking for a source to get in front of more than 100,000 people (and PR agencies). Think about that for a second and how smart it is. It solves problems for both audiences, the media who needs sources and stories and the people who need to get the word out about their business or brand. HARO matches them together through a daily e-mail, allowing them to contact each other independently of the system. Brilliant!

Imagine you needed to find sources to interview for the eBook you're writing on Content Management Solutions (CMS). You would use HARO to find experts or contacts in that field, free! Those experts would then contact you on their own and voila, you have saved yourself countless hours of research. On the flip side, everyone, and that means you, should be signed up for HARO to receive the daily e-mails. You never know when someone is going to post a query to the list looking for information on a topic in which you are an expert.

In fact, I used HARO to do research for this book. Many of the stories you read here were from HARO subscribers. In exchange for their input, they will receive publicity that they never would have gotten before, all for sending me an e-mail with their story, and saving me countless hours of research time.

If you've ever seen Mr. Shankman speak you would most likely have heard his *Titanic* story. Here's my attempt to tell it as best as I can remember. It's a great example of picking up on a hot trend and turning that into attention and sales:

The year was 1998 and I was in the process of starting my own business, but I needed some money to get it done. In 1998, the blockbuster smash movie *Titanic* came out on video. Do you remember the buzz around the movie when it was released? You couldn't turn on the television or any media and not hear about it, and now the video was arriving and the buzz was picking up again. I thought to myself, "what a great opportunity to see if I could make some money and get some publicity from all this excitement." Therefore, I came up with a t-shirt that said, "It Sank. Get Over It." I had 500 shirts printed up out of my own money and headed down to Times Square in New York City not knowing what to expect. Five hours later, I had sold every single one of those shirts for $15 a piece.

After that epic sales day, I really thought I was onto something. Therefore, I decided to cold call a reporter at *USA Today*. I told her about my t-shirts and how I sold them all in one day. She asked if I had a place to sell them online and I said yes and gave her the homemade web site I had constructed. The next day my story and URL was mentioned in the newspaper, which then got picked up by all kinds of media, helping me sell thousands more t-shirts, and putting enough funds in my bank account to create my own firm called The Geek Factory, Inc.

While HARO is a monumental success in its own right, Mr. Shankman has also engineered some of the most outrageous attention-getting PR stunts in modern-day history. Following are a few more stories from which you might find some inspiration.

Throw the CEO from the Plane!

To help get attention for his new PR firm, Mr. Shankman organized a group skydive of 100 CEO's, dot-com workers, and media figures. The buzz from the event helped launch his firm's brand name out to millions of potential customers, landing him many new accounts, and a lot of media contacts to boot.

Giant Balls of Yarn!

A small yarn shop in upstate New York hired the Geek Factory to get the word out about them. How did they do it? Easy. Buy a transport van and manufacture two gigantic balls of yarn to mount on top of it. Then use that van to drive customers to and from the yarn store.

Free Domain Names!

Registerfree.com needed to find a way to stand out from the other big domain name registration services. So why not give away free domain names for an hour on a given day and time? Great idea, until the promotion's success virtually shut down Internet access on the East Coast for more than nine hours.

As you can see, public relations are closely associated with the art of getting attention. Actually, you could say that getting attention is one of the basic concepts of the beginning of the public relations strategy. However, not every PR strategy is focused on an attention-getting stunt. A successful PR strategy definitely goes beyond that, and extends much further.

9

Mark Cuban Hates Me

IF YOU DON'T know who Mark Cuban is, he's the billionaire entrepreneur owner of the Dallas Mavericks of the National Basketball Association (NBA). Mr. Cuban wasn't always a billionaire mind you. He made his success by selling his very successful web site, Broadcast.com to Yahoo! for $5.9 billion, yes, I said billion, in 1999 during the dot-com days. The point I'm trying to make is this guy is a billionaire. For you and me, and well everybody, getting in touch with a billionaire is not something very easy to do.

As an avid reader of Mr. Cuban's blog (www.blogmaverick .com), and a fan of his in general, I came up with the idea one day to see if I could get him to call me. No, not a way for me to find out how to call him, but rather, a way to get *him* to call *me*. The year was 2006, way before things like Facebook and Twitter existed as they are today. Sure, the Internet still existed and it was in general easier to try and find contact information for most everyone, but still, you couldn't just go to Google and find someone's home phone number and e-mail address.

Besides, my goal was to get him to call me, not the other way around. The first thing I did was buy a domain name called www .markcubanpleasecallme.com. On that web site, I wrote a simple letter.

Today is Monday, April 10, 2006 and I am launching this new blog site to see if I can get Mark Cuban to call me at 1-888-BLOG-BIZ (256-4249).

The clock starts today. How long will it take Mark to see this web site and call me? Only time will tell!

WHY DO I WANT MARK CUBAN TO CALL ME?

I don't really have anything interesting to say to Mark. I do like his "maverick" style, and admire his success and thought-leadership; however, I don't have any business plan to pitch to him, or anything like that. This is an experiment. I want to see if I can use a quickly made blog and some cheap blog promotion techniques to get Mark to **call me at 1-888-BLOG-BIZ.**

WHAT'S THE POINT?

I think Mark will appreciate this as a blogging proponent and all-around smart guy. The point is to prove further the powerful nature of instant publishing/blogging. If I can use this blog and a simple press release to get the attention of a person like Mark Cuban, and then actually get him to call me, I can further prove that blogging is indeed a powerful way to get attention and get your thoughts out there, cheaply and quickly.

EXACTLY HOW ARE YOU PROMOTING THIS?

I want to do as little promotion as possible. So I've made this typepad powered blog as Step 1. Then the only other thing

I'm going to do is release a press release to Prweb.com at the $80 level (release gets sent out on Wednesday, April 12). I'm hoping that the release, using the proper keywords (Mark Cuban) in the title, will eventually get blogged by other people and possibly get put in front of Mark himself via a news alert from either Google or Yahoo!. I repeat, I am not going to tell anybody about this web site, or even link to it from any of my other blogs. As far as the world knows, this blog will be hidden to everyone and they will have to find it themselves.

WHO AM I?

My name is Jim Kukral and I'm a long-time blogger/Internet marketer who wants to continue to prove the power of blogging through unique and fun experiments like this. If you care to read my bio, you can do so here.

Mark Cuban, Please Call Me at 1-888-BLOG-BIZ (256-4249).

That was it. As the letter stated, I did not tell one single person, not even my wife, about it. I wrote up a simple press release and sent it out "on the wire" through Prweb.com and waited to be contacted. I wasn't sure if I would be, but again, this was all an experiment. The day after the release "hit the wire," I received a phone call from a reporter at the *Dallas Morning News* who had seen my release and wanted to interview me for a story. Remember, this was 2006, the "wire" still kinda worked.

Tip: When a reporter calls . . . always find the time to take it.

I dropped everything I was doing and agreed to the interview. It turns out the reporter was assigned to the Mark Cuban beat, which had lead him to monitor the news wire for all things related to that name. I answered a bunch of questions about my idea, thanked him, and went back to my regular day, not really thinking I would ever hear from him again. A few hours later I received a call back from the reporter informing me that, "I just spoke to Mark, and he said he hates you."

Shock! Hates me? What did I do? I was flabbergasted for a moment, until I realized that what I had done had almost worked. I was able to get my name put in front of a billionaire in less than two days. Success! As it turned out after discussing it with the reporter, Mark apparently had some other person named Jim who had been writing bad things about him online for years, and he confused that person with me, so he didn't really hate me. The next day the story ran in the paper. Still no call from Mark. Not that it mattered to me, I had somewhat accomplished my goal.

Here's where it gets good. Mr. Cuban now knows who I am. A month went by and I realized that he wasn't going to call me. That's when plan B went into effect. Instead of getting him to call me, I wanted to see now if he'd know who I was and respond to me. I sent out an e-mail to him (he lists his e-mail on his blog) telling him who I was and reminding him of the story. Fifteen minutes later, I get an e-mail back from him laughing about the story and congratulating me on generating press and getting his attention.

Win! Technically, no, he never did call me. However, I did get his attention, and have since turned that attention into the following successes for my business and myself:

- My company at the time, Blogkits, worked with his movie studio, Magnolia Pictures, on a project together.
- I was asked to introduce him at the Blogworld Expo event, where I was able to stand with him on stage and introduce him to the crowd of thousands where I told this story.

- My blog received thousands of new visitors from telling this story.
- He provided me a speaking testimonial that I use on my promotional materials that helps qualify me to potential customers. He also wrote a back cover blurb for this book.
- A billionaire answers my e-mails, talks to me, and gives me advice from time to time.

10

New Jersey Man Sells Brooklyn Bridge . . . for $14.95!

ACCORDING TO PAUL Hartunian, "Every person on this planet can get tremendous amounts of free publicity for any product, service, cause, or issue. They just have to be taught the simple steps to take . . . and then take them." If you've never heard of Paul by name that's okay, you've probably heard of him as the guy who literally sold the Brooklyn Bridge for only $14.95. Maybe you saw him on CNN, *Paul Harvey News*, the *New York Times*, the *Regis Philbin Show*, *Smart Money*, *Forbes* magazine, *New Jersey Monthly*, *Money* magazine, *USA Today*, the *Wall Street Journal*, and more than 1,000 other radio and TV talk shows? Regardless of how you have heard of him, or not, Paul knows how to get attention for himself and his clients.

Paul's greatest claim to fame is the Brooklyn Bridge story. It goes that he heard that some parts of the Brooklyn Bridge were being dismantled and replaced with new parts. Specifically, the old wooden pedestrian walkway. What Paul did was work out a deal with the demolition crew to buy the old scraps of rotted wood for $500. Then he had the wood cut up into 1" square pieces, each about $\frac{1}{8}$" thick. Okay, so the plan was to sell the wood, we all get it. However, how do you go about getting attention for the plan so you can actually make sales? You could spend thousands of dollars on advertising and hope the message would get out, or . . .

Paul wrote a press release with the title "New Jersey Man Sells Brooklyn Bridge . . . for $14.95!" He then created an official looking certificate and prepared some history about the Brooklyn Bridge for the packet. Then he wrote, "Attached to this certificate is a genuine piece of the original wooden pedestrian walkway of the Brooklyn Bridge." At the top of the certificate, he drew a small box where the piece of wood was going to be attached. The next day he mailed out a press packet to key media contacts and waited. The whole thing cost him less than $100 to prepare and mail.

A few days later Paul's phone wouldn't stop ringing. Reporters, not just local, but national, were coming to his door wanting to interview him. Newspapers, magazines, radio and television shows wanted him to come on and talk about his idea. It was a huge attention-getting success, even landing him an appearance on *The Tonight Show* with Johnny Carson.

11

One Video Got My Message Through

About 3 years ago, I became a big believer in the future of online video. The rise of YouTube had me convinced that online video was a smart business opportunity not only for me, but also for service firms who wanted to offer video services. The writing was on the wall, consumers were becoming less and less open to traditional marketing messages like banners and web sites, and instead were responding more to multimedia messages like audio and video. Therefore, I knew that I wanted to be a part of that trend, but I didn't have the startup funds to go out and create the Web video company that I had envisioned. Actually, I knew I didn't want to own that type of business; I just wanted to be part of one and help create one. Hey, I like working for myself.

I still had many connections with former partners and associates in the Web space, and I figured it would be best to try to convince one of them about the future of Web video and get them to put in the money and let me create a business for them that they could run. The problem was that YouTube was still relatively new and many of my contacts didn't yet understand how online video could be worked into a business strategy.

Therefore, I needed a way to make them understand, and the best way to do that is to show them exactly what I already knew.

One of the people I used to be in business with was the president of a top-15 search engine firm with more than 50 employees. I identified this person and company as someone who would be perfect to pitch my idea to, and then went about proving to them that my idea was indeed a good one. No, I didn't call them and pitch, nor did I e-mail them, or drop by in person for a meeting. I took a different tack, one that was sure to get their attention.

The concept was simple and the pitch even simpler. I created a short video of myself explaining the business idea to the president of the firm. Then I uploaded the video to YouTube and made sure to tag the video with the President's name and company name. Then I waited a few days to give YouTube some time to index the video. After that, I sent an e-mail to the person that said simply, "Do me a favor, go to YouTube and search for your name. Then ring me back if you're interested in talking some more about it." I didn't pitch the idea at all, or give any more details.

He did, and guess what happened? The video I made showed up as the number-one result. He watched the video, got my message, saw how powerful it was to have a video as a message and called me back in less than an hour. The next day I was in his office negotiating a deal that would bring me on board as a contractor to create and run his brand-new Web video department. The whole thing took about an hour of my time.

If you're trying to get the attention of one person, think about using creative ways to get it done. You'll find that more than 50 percent of the battle is getting the person to notice you and pay attention. After you've done that, wow them with your skill and knowledge, then watch as you might just get what you were after.

Don't Send a Letter, Make a Video!

If you want to get the attention of somebody, or a business, in today's busy world, you should make a video. Phone calls don't work anymore, usually. Letters . . . who opens them? Just ask Darren Bryant of Pensacola, Florida. Darren spent hours in what he calls Bank of America's phone maze, being bounced from person to person, never reaching somebody who could address his situation.

Enough was enough, and Darren needed his problem resolved so he took one more shot at getting the attention of someone who could help him. He created a five-minute video of his situation and uploaded it to YouTube. In the video, he gives his phone number and e-mail address and says, "The reason I'm making this video is to get in contact with somebody from Bank of America that can make a decision." He then e-mailed a link of the video to over a dozen Bank of America e-mail addresses he said he found online.

Four hours later Darren received a phone call from a high-level executive with the bank who took his information and started an investigation into the matter. Darren's story is not unique either. Consumers are turning to the video card by the hundreds of thousands, putting constant pressure on the necks of the big companies who, for too long of a time, have chosen to provide poor customer service.

Don't send a letter, make a video.

12

The Million-Dollar Question!

I'M OFTEN PUT on the spot either in a business meeting with a client, on stage speaking to a live audience, or on Ustream (live video) with the question that goes something like this: "Okay Jim, so how do I make money once I have the attention?"

Um . . . If only it was that easy.

Ideas

It's ironic that I'm writing a book on the topic of getting attention to drive revenue and publicity, yet when put to the test in a business meeting or social situation, I'm often out of ideas on the spot. People seem to think that attention-getting ideas just fall out of the sky and into your head and vomit out of your mouth in an exorcist type of way.

Quite the opposite is true. There's a reason why only a certain amount of people and businesses excel at getting attention and that is because it's hard.

As Seth Godin mentions in his inspiring book, *The Dip*, if you can get through the dip, in other words, the hard part, then you can rise to the top of the curve, and that's where excellence happens. That's when average becomes remarkable. In addition, when you become remarkable, the money has a much better chance of flowing your way. The bad news is that coming up with the idea is the hard part. We all can't just come up with the greatest, smartest, most inspiring, intelligent, attention-getting idea at the drop of a hat all the time.

The good news is that it's learnable. If you follow the right exercises and learn the right way to think, you're more able to be that genius, bright shining star that customers will want to work with or your boss will want to promote.

13

---

26 Ways to Generate Killer Ideas

SO YOU HEAR about all of these people making money with great ideas, and you think, "Well, it's easy for them, but I'm not creative. I could never come up with ideas like those." Wrong! Generating ideas—useful ideas—is a skill and, like any other skill, it can be learned. The more you practice, the easier it will be to come up with ideas whenever you need them. Whether you are looking for a new business concept, ways to improve your products and services, or strategies to get attention for yourself and your business, the techniques here will help you. Try them and see which ones work best for you.

1. *Get in the idea mind-set.* Although you can learn to generate ideas on demand, if you are always on the lookout for ideas you will never run out of them.
2. *Carry a notebook or recorder at all times.* The only thing worse than not being able to come up with an idea is thinking of an amazing idea, not writing it down and then forgetting it. You may think you will remember, but you won't. Having a small notepad or digital recorder with you at all times guarantees that those ideas will not escape.

3. *Eavesdrop.* Listen to people talking on the bus, at the coffee shop, or in the elevator. Build on the snippets of conversation you overhear to create a story, and let that story lead you to a brilliant idea.

4. *Do something new.* Sign up for a class, take up a new hobby, listen to a different kind of music, or do anything that is new to you. You'll get new parts of your brain humming, meet new people, and get new ideas.

5. *Hold a grudge.* What annoys you? Chances are it also annoys other people. Keep track of the things that bug you and find a way to make them better.

6. *Forget everything you know.* Too often, we let our biases creep in and influence our thinking. Start fresh, without preconceived notions of what you *must* do or what is *impossible.* Be open to anything and everything.

7. *Combine things in interesting ways.* Take two ideas and put them together to make one new idea. After all, what is a Snuggie but the mutation of a blanket and a robe? Go beyond obvious connections to come up with something truly innovative.

8. *Give advice to someone else.* Sometimes we are too close to a situation to see the best solution. Imagine that someone else is coming to you with the problem you are trying to solve. What would you tell them?

9. *Get physical.* Movement increases the flow of endorphins, as well as sending more blood to your brain. Okay, I'm not a doctor and I don't play one on TV, so maybe I don't have all the physical stuff exactly right. However, I know that getting active helps me think. I keep a mini-trampoline in my office and jump up and down for a few minutes to get my blood moving. Run, skip, jump, climb stairs, or otherwise get your pulse rate up to get your brain moving, too.

10. *Have people ask you questions.* Get someone who is not familiar with your situation to ask you questions about it. They may ask things that lead you to an idea that you overlooked because it was too obvious.

11. *Listen.* Really listen when customers talk to you. You will hear ideas for new products and services, ways to improve customer service, and uses you never considered for your products that can open up new markets for you. Chances are that your customers will not recognize when they are giving you ideas, but you need to be able to spot them. Are several customers making the same comments or asking the same questions? Act on it! I have gotten six-figure ideas this way.

12. *Do the opposite.* If something isn't working, consider doing exactly the opposite of what you are doing. It might work!

13. *Doodle.* Make random doodles on a white board or a piece of paper. Draw, jot words, make circles, or whatever you do when you doodle. As you loosen up, ideas may start to form on the page.

14. *Change your routine.* Drive a new route to the office, try a new restaurant for lunch, start work a little earlier (or a little later), work in a different place, or anything that busts you out of your rut. New surroundings and new experiences can help you think differently.

15. *Listen to music.* You may find that a little Mozart awakens your creativity, or you may respond better to Metallica. Whatever works for you. Fire up your iPod, get into the groove, and let your mind work.

16. *Take a shower.* How many great ideas do you get in the shower? It's not a coincidence that great thinking happens in the shower. Showering is a mindless activity (the only thing you really have to think about is, "Have I already repeated, or just lathered and rinsed?") and the warm water is relaxing. Let your mind wander and you may come up with a brilliant idea.

17. *Walk the dog.* Grab the leash and take Rover for a walk around the block or through the park. The exercise, fresh air, and sunshine are good for both of you, and it could help at least one of you to think better.

18. *Make a list.* This always works for me. Get out a notepad, or fire up your computer, and write down everything you can

think of related to your issue. For example, if you need a slogan for a product, write down every feature and benefit you can think of, the types of people who need the product, the problems it solves, and so on. Pull out a thesaurus and start looking up synonyms. When you are done, you will not only have your slogan, you will have a library of words and phrases you can use in your marketing and publicity campaigns.

19. *Wear a silly hat.* Use a prop when it is time to be creative. It could be anything (such as wearing a silly hat) that signals to your brain that it is time to go into idea-generating mode. Have a routine that you follow when you want to be creative. It might be to put on your hat, grab a ball to toss up in the air, and lean back in your chair with your feet on the desk. Once you are in your "Creative at Work" position, start coming up with ideas. Do this a few times, and you will be conditioned to start generating ideas as soon as you see the hat. Your brain will have been trained.

20. *Read everything.* Read business books, novels, newspapers, magazines, blogs, and everything else. The more raw materials you take in, the better you will become at putting together seemingly unrelated concepts to create something new.

21. *Sleep on it.* Just before going to bed, think about the ideas you want to generate. Be specific: "I will come up with great ways to promote our new widget." Tell yourself you will come up with a solution while you sleep. Keep a pad and pen or a recorder next to your bed so you can capture the ideas as soon as you wake up.

22. *Go to Google.* Enter a few words related to the idea you are looking for. Google will try to automatically complete your query, and may come up with just what you need. Then look at some of the search results to see what inspires you.

23. *Get a little help from your friends.* Bring together a few of your creative friends and colleagues for a brainstorming session. Start throwing ideas around and be willing to be silly.

Sometimes the best ideas sound a little crazy at first. Record the session so no one has to slow down to take notes. Oh, and having a pitcher of margaritas on hand can help the ideas flow more readily.

24. *Hire a professional.* Many of my clients come to me for help in getting ideas for their businesses. Sometimes I come up with ideas for them, but often my role is simply to help them find the great ideas that are buried in their brains. A consultant can ask the right questions to steer you to the idea you need.

25. *Borrow an idea.* Everyone thinks that their business is not like anyone else's. The truth is that all of our businesses are more alike than different. Look at what others are doing in other industries and see how you can apply their ideas. By the time you adapt their idea to precisely fit your business it will be unique.

26. *Start creating "it."* You do not have to wait until a concept is fully formed to take your first action. Begin with the germ of an idea and start developing it. As you do, you will discover the problems as well as the opportunities and you will be able to refine your idea as you go.

Use these techniques whenever you need ideas and you will discover that the more you use your creative abilities, the better they will become.

Cathy Stucker is the Idea Lady. Her business model is "Learn it, do it, teach it," and she has taught thousands of people to replicate her success in publishing, publicity, creating passive income, and other ventures. Cathy has appeared on radio and television programs from coast to coast, and has been featured in the *New York Times,* the *Houston Chronicle, Black Enterprise,* the Associated Press, *Startup Journal* (*Wall Street Journal*), CNN.com, *Woman's Day,* and many other publications. Get more great ideas from Cathy at http://www.IdeaLady.com

If you're like me, you have lots of ideas, some good and some bad, but some great! Oftentimes I'll pull an idea out from years before and end up using it on some new project for a client or myself. It's important for you to create a list of ideas that you have and keep that list of ideas near you at all times. You've heard of writers who carry a notepad with them at all times to jot down notes or ideas for stories, right? The same applies here.

Post-it Notes Resume

I was fresh out of college and on yet another entry-level job interview. This time it was for an advertising agency in Akron, Ohio. Upon walking into the CEO's office, I noticed the walls completely covered in Post-it notes. Being the inquisitive type that I am, I asked him what all the notes were about. He told me he liked to keep his ideas and notes in this manner, saying it helped him stay organized and kept the ideas in front of his face. Not thinking much of it at the time, I went home and told my wife—my fiancée at the time—the story. When retelling the story to her, I had my very own idea. My goal was to get the job, so why not use this guy's penchant for Post-it notes to get me to stand out to him. I'm not naive; I realized that I wasn't the best designer in the world, and that they were most likely interviewing many other candidates.

So I went to the local store and bought a big piece of white-poster board and several packs of yellow Post-it notes. I then came up with about fifty different qualities that I represented. You know, stuff such as "hard working" or "intelligent" or "highly-skilled," and so on. I had my fiancée, who has fabulous hand-writing, write down each quality on a single Post-it note. Then we took all the notes and stuck them to the poster-board one by one, emulating the CEO's office wall.

The next morning I arrived at his office early. He wasn't in yet, so I left the posterboard with all of the Post-it notes on it with his receptionist and another copy of my résumé. I must say she looked at me quite funny, but that's what you get when you do things differently. About an hour later, I received a call from the CEO offering me the job. I was right! Out of all the people interviewing for the position, I was the only one who did something to stand out. This was an early and valuable lesson for me and has since helped shape my career and brand into what it is today.

Of course, Post-it notes can work, but they can become unwieldy for sure. What are some other ways to keep track of your ideas? I have more than 2,000 "friends" on Facebook and just over 20,000 followers on Twitter. I decided to ask this question on Twitter and Facebook and here are some responses:

How do you keep track of your ideas and notes? I'm including your responses in my book—Posted on @jimkukral Twitter

- Patrick R. Riccards said on Facebook, Everything I write is on 3 × 5 cards. Keep them in all of my suits. Then can organize notes and thoughts however I need later.
- @beley on Twitter said, Evernote (Mac & iPhone). Great for jotting down ideas. Later I add them to OmniFocus to my "One Day/Maybe" folder.
- Evan Weber said on Facebook, iphone notes app.
- Carmen Sakurai said on Facebook, Voice notes!
- Michael Temple on Facebook said, Notebook.
- Jane Velz Kurko on Facebook said, Old school, black and white "Composition Books"—several of them, and in no particular order. Occasional scraps of paper and backs of envelopes, which get put into those books. But mostly, in my head.
- Brandon Hoffman on Facebook said, I keep my ideas in my iphone. Since I always have the phone on me, I whip it out when I come up with an idea and make a note.

- @HowToMakeMyBlog on Twitter said, I recently moved from evernote to Google docs for keeping my notes and ideas, it works perfectly, I don't need anything else.
- @Ahmetkirtok on Twitter said, iPhone notes (especially when I'm traveling), Gmail, and Project Management.
- @davidjacobs on Twitter said, Notes in the cloud. My ideas have to flow with me. For now Evernote is my fav cloud note keeper.
- Teddy Carroll said on Facebook, I have three different places depending on what I'm capturing: (1) I capture all of my writing and photography ideas in a notebook—usually composition or moleskine; (2) All InterWebs stuff is captured in Google Notebook for a quick look up; (3) General ideas, lists, gifts . . . you know, walking around stuff is captured on my Palm Pre with an app . . . See Morecalled Memo. It looks like little Post-It notes on a corkboard. I usually know where to look for ideas because I try to keep the things cataloged unique to the medium.
- Ginette Degner said on Facebook, I carry a small leather bound book a bit smaller than my checkbook. It is small enough I can take it anywhere to write down my ideas. I keep them all and at the end of the year I go through them. I have also been known to register domains using GoDaddy and my iphone when I get a great idea before the ink is even dry.
- Sandra Roussel said on Facebook, I use TextPad and jot down my ideas, when I turn on the puter TextPad is opened second after my e-mail program. When on the run, I use the note application on my cell phone.
- Vinny Ohare said on Facebook, My ideas get stored on my android phone using notepad then uploaded to computer using helipad.

I used to have a Word document on my desktop that is only for ideas but I've now switched to Google Docs (Docs.google.com) so it's accessible anytime, anywhere. The important thing is that it's there at a moment's notice, allowing me to go in, add to it, and review it. This document holds some of the most creative thoughts I've ever had. I've never shown it to anyone, nor will I as it contains ideas that might seem silly to other people, but I value it greatly as a place where I can think freely and creatively without criticism.

That's truly the key to coming up with great ideas. You need to free yourself from worry about what other people might say. If you have a place where you can brainstorm and record some of your most outrageous thoughts for getting attention without having to worry about someone else laughing at you, then you'll find that it's much easier to be creative, and well, outrageous.

14

Three Truths to Coming up with Great Ideas

DON THE IDEA Guy lives, breathes, and sleeps in the world of ideas. Here's three of his secrets to generating ideas that matter. You can learn more about Don by visiting DontheIdeaGuy.com.

1. *I come up with a lot of good ideas because I come up with a lot of bad ideas.* I ran across this quote by Linus Pauling early on in my life and fully believed it: "The best way to come up with a good idea is to come up with a lot of ideas." It's purely a numbers game. If I come up with more ideas (bad ideas, crazy ideas, old ideas, new ideas, outrageous ideas, safe ideas, dangerous ideas, half-baked ideas, out of this world ideas, scary ideas, unreasonable ideas, any and all kinds of ideas) than other people, I will also come up with more good ideas than other people.
2. *I make room for more ideas.* Most people can come up with one or two ideas that they think are really, really good. I mean,

they absolutely feel this is a *gonna make me rich, rich, rich* idea. Alternatively, they have the opposite problem—they get these ideas that they feel are below average, they don't really stand out, probably already been thought-up by someone else, and so on. The problem is, that in both cases, either the individual expends incredible amounts of mental energy trying to retain their brilliant idea, or the less-than-brilliant idea swims around in their head as they try to come up with something cleverer. The solution to either of these situations is the same—record the idea on paper (in some sort of permanent idea journal) so the brain knows the idea has been safely tucked away for future reference, and free up your mental matter so it can expend energy on coming up with the *next* idea.

3. *I constantly fuel my brain.* If you're going to treat your brain as an engine, you have to make sure it has premium fuel to burn when you step on the gas pedal. I read books, magazines, blogs, comic books, and so on *constantly* on the widest variety of subjects. I watch TV and movies, all genres. I listen to music (again, all genres), visit art museums, the ballet, stare at stars, do crossword puzzles, play video games, write business articles, write fictional short stories, keep a journal, sketch and doodle, go to comedy clubs, attend seminars, speak at seminars, drive the long way to work, find short cuts home from work, go to the zoo, visit coffee shops, try new restaurants, ride a motorcycle, play golf, darts, billiards, have passionate conversations (and sometimes arguments!) with friends, and probably fifty other things that I can't even recall right this second. The really important thing is that while I am feeding my brain all of these experiences, my radar is always *up* to draw a parallel or find a metaphor that matches whatever projects or problems on which I may be working at the time. The rest of the information simply gets stored into my mental database of information, so that it's there to be called upon whenever I have need.

15

DO Think Outside of the Box and What Can Happen When You Do

ALL THIS TALK of ideas is making me hungry! FancyFastFood.com is an out-of-the-box idea that definitely gets your attention. They take fast food and turn it into gourmet looking food, then take pictures of it and post it on their web site. Head on over and take a look at how you can turn a Chipotle burrito into Chicken Chipotlioli, or how to turn Wendy's Hash Browns into Bubbe Wendy's Hanukkah Latkes.

Like you, I'm tired of hearing we need to be *out of the box*. However, as seen from the example of FancyFastFood.com, being *out of the box* can work. What are you doing to think outside the box? Don't discredit it. Try to live it and work with it, then see what happens. You just might be surprised at what you come up with that succeeds beyond your wildest dreams.

Why Didn't I Think of That?

Inevitably, at some point in your life you've had a head-slapping, stop in your tracks moment where you say to yourself, "Why didn't I think of that?" Every year thousands of people come up with a new product, or service, or web site idea that makes it big, earning the creator either a giant paycheck, a boatload of publicity, or both.

So why isn't that person you? It can be. We've already talked about ways you can bring out your inner creativity through the power of idea creation. You're primed now and ready to go and hopefully already have a stack of ideas in your head that you can move on.

Now what? Well, now it's time to act! Still not ready? Maybe you just need to hear about some people who have done it in order to get your juices flowing. Following is a rundown of some of those people who took their ideas (crazy as they may seem) and turned them into gold.

Jason Sadler is another one of those Web-entrepreneurs that have taken a silly or creative idea and turned it into Web gold! Jason created IwearYourShirt.com, a site that features him wearing a new shirt every day, each one sponsored by a new advertiser. In 2009, Jason successfully sold 365 days of sponsored shirt wearing, earning him just under $70,000.

Yes, you read that right. Jason made almost $70,000 for wearing a different t-shirt every day. Doesn't sound so silly now, does it? Listen to an exclusive interview of how Jason did it at AttentiontheBook.com.

Kyle MacDonald bartered his way from a single red paperclip to a house in a series of online trades over the course of a year. That's right; he used the power of the Internet and a creative idea to trade something of almost zero value, for something (a house) of actual real value.

Alex Tew is the guy who came up with The Million Dollar Homepage. A student at the time, Tew needed to find a way to pay for his education, so he took a chance and created a web page that sold 1,000,000 pixels for $1 each. Hence, "The Million Dollar Homepage." In fact, Tew did sell all 1 million pixels and earned himself a nice paycheck, and tons of publicity in the process.

These projects illustrate that even the simplest or craziest, weirdest, unusual idea can be turned into reality and Web gold. It should also be pointed out that for every one of these types of projects that succeed, ninety-nine other similar projects never get off the ground. Personally, I've taken two stabs at viral glory with two web sites that never did catch on. If you want to see them in action visit AwesomeMillion.com and BigBrownBox.com.

Just because success doesn't come doesn't mean you should stop trying. As all-time great Wayne Gretzky so famously quoted once, "You miss 100 percent of the shots you don't take."

For inspiration, here's a quick list of some risk-takers you probably know about that turned an idea into reality and into a huge success.

- Red Bull energy drink. The idea was to create a super-caffeinated carbonated beverage and market it to athletes and the party crowd. Through some creative and unusual advertising, Red Bull now has $3.4 billion in sales.
- Amazon.com. Who wants to have to go to a bookstore to buy a book? Jeff Bezos created Amazon because he realized that driving to the bookstore was an enormous hassle and there could be a better way.
- Polo. Ralph Lauren thought to himself, "What if we take a regular polo shirt, and add a little horse decal on it and price it at $50?" In 1994, he sold 28 percent of the company to Goldman Sachs for $138 million.

16

Do You Market Outrageously?

GREAT MARKETERS KNOW that in order to get someone to pay attention to them, they have to find ways to generate a reaction from them. Good or bad, it doesn't really matter, without some kind, any kind, of reaction you're not going to be remembered. In the early days on the Web, marketers made brightly-colored and fast-moving, blinking banner ads to get the reader to pay attention. While that worked at first, readers quickly became weary of such an in-your-face style. Today, banner ads, blinking or not, have become pretty much ineffective as a whole. The point is that what may have worked once, might not work forever.

Your business struggles every day to get the attention of potential customers. Why? Because you're doing it wrong. The traditional and conservative marketing attempts you've been using just aren't working anymore. Writing a check to your local radio station for a series of promo spots on the morning zoo show doesn't work as well as it used to. Buying a classified ad in the local newspaper doesn't yield you the quantity or quality of job applicants that you used to get. Combine those things with the fact that while those things don't work as well as they used to, they still cost just as much.

Sometimes, just maybe, you'd be better off thinking a little bit outrageously, to take you off that losing cycle of slow growth and average returns for your business that you've justified as the best we can do. However, it's not the best you can do. Being adequate and shooting for *some* success is no way to run a business. The time is now to start thinking big, and a little bit outrageously. How else are you truly ever going to make that leap to the next level?

You Don't Sell Blank

Perhaps the first step in figuring out how to think outrageously is first to understand that you're not selling what you think you're selling. For example, Nike doesn't sell golf balls and sports apparel. Nike sells winning. That's why you see the biggest winners in the world, like Tiger Woods and Lebron James, representing their brand. DeBeers doesn't sell diamonds. DeBeers sells "forever." You aren't buying a diamond, you can get one of those from anyone, you're buying a "lifetime."

Most businesses today think they're selling something that they're really not. Think about what you sell, really think about it. Chances are you have the sales pitch wrong. Try to get inside the head of your potential customer and understand what pain you are taking away from them. If you're a tax service, you're not selling someone to do their taxes; you're selling things such as a safeguard from the IRS or relief from the stress and anxiety of doing your taxes. In other words, you're selling them freedom from their fear of doing something wrong, and the pain and inconvenience they used to feel when they did their taxes themselves.

Here's some space below to try this exercise. Write in your answers.

I Don't Sell _____, I Sell _____.

Here are some examples to help get you rolling:

- I Don't Sell Office Furniture, I Sell Equipment to Create Comfort and Productivity in the Workplace!
- I Don't Sell Productivity Software, I Sell Helping People Get More Done in Less Time!
- I Don't Sell Lawn Mowers, I Sell Powerful Tools That Help People Make Their Yards Beautiful!

Sports marketers get this. They know that they're not selling sports; they're selling entertainment. You take your kids or your brother out to a game because it's fun, it's something to do, and you want to be entertained. The truth is that only a small percentage of people in the world really give a darn about sports. Therefore, if you want to fill a stadium nightly, you have to go after the people who want something more than sports.

Mike Veeck, author of *Fun Is Good*, has been fired by four major league baseball teams in his career because he knew that in order to keep a stadium full of people, you have to sell more than sports, and you also have to think a little bit outrageously. As with most wild card thinkers like Veeck, that kind of attitude and thinking usually doesn't play to well to a room full of unimaginative stuffed-suits. Too bad for them. Veeck is the guy who is responsible for the infamous disco-demolition event with the White Sox back in the 1970s. While that event ended up being a bit of a disaster for him and the organization, it certainly lives in infamy as a memorable event.

Veeck is now the coowner of six minor league baseball teams spread around the country. He continues to fill the stands by practicing marketing tactics that shock and amaze. Here's a partial list of some of the real events he's put together:

- On Tonya Harding Mini-Bat Night with the Charleston RiverDogs, fans received a miniature bat and the former figure skater was on hand to autograph them.

- On Vasectomy Night with the Charleston RiverDogs, fans came to the game on Father's Day and had a chance to win a free vasectomy. The event was canceled at the last minute because a religious figure called MLB headquarters to voice his displeasure and they were forced to cancel the promo.
- On Enron Night with the Portland Beavers, paper shredders were placed at the gates and the announced attendance was found to be inflated and later adjusted downward. They announced 238k, which was way off.
- On Mime-O-Vision Night with the St. Paul Saints, five mimes acted out plays atop the dugout while 6,329 stared in stupefaction. Concession sales were strong, but staff had to escort the mimes out after fans hurled hot dogs at the actors. "The fans couldn't believe what they were seeing," said Veeck. "It was the best night we ever had in St. Paul. The game was held up for 20 minutes while the fans threw hot dogs at the mimes, they hated them."
- On Silent Night with the Charleston RiverDogs—originally created by one of the minority owners, celebrity Bill Murray—fans taped their mouths and sat in silence, using signs to cheer, boo, and get the beer man's attention. Librarians served as ushers. "My favorite is the little girl who held up the sign that said I have to pee," said Veeck.
- On Nobody Night with the Charleston RiverDogs, the 1,800 fans that showed up were locked out of the stadium for a tailgate party until the fifth inning, when the game became official. Announced attendance: zero. We figured out the lowest attendance was one for a minor league game, so we went after the record. "After the Nobody Night we did 125 interviews all over the world," said Veeck. "We were grabbing fans and having them do interviews because we didn't have enough staff. It was a huge hit."

So why do these things? Because they get attention and drive revenue. A day after the Nobody Night event, a local businessman walked into Veeck's office with a check for $50,000 offering to be the sponsor for the next one. Now that's results. When was the last time an advertiser found you and begged you to spend their money? "We sent out a press release saying we were going to do an event called a 'Salute to Duct Tape' for the Tampa Bay Devil Rays," said Veeck. "The next day we got a call from one of the major manufacturers of Duct Tape in Cleveland, Ohio. They had seen the story in their local paper and wanted to know how they could sponsor the event. We flew them down, negotiated a deal, and took their check."

One of my favorite marketing books of all time is *Marketing Outrageously* written by Jon Spoelstra. Like Veeck, Spoelstra pretty much invented the concepts and strategies of outrageous sports marketing. His philosophy is, "What's it going to take to _____." In other words, if you want to see big results, you need to think big—like walking into a room and saying things such as, "What's it going to take to sell out every game this year?" or "What's it going to take to get every season ticket holder to renew this year?"

When the Sacramento Kings brought in Spolestra, he was tasked with getting season ticket holders to renew. The problem was that the team was bad, and it was harder than ever to even get fans to open the mail they were being sent. He knew he had written a great letter and offer and that if it was read, would get them to renew. So what do you do to *make sure* they would open the letter? Easy. Send rubber chickens.

He went out and bought a truckload of three-foot-long rubber chickens, put a jersey on them and attached a note that said "Don't Fowl Out!" The rubber chicken was stuffed into a tubular FedEx container and mailed to fans. As Spoelstra explains, the FedEx box was the headline and the rubber chicken was the subheadline. The only purpose of the headline is to get the prospect to read the subheadline. The purpose of the subheadline is to get the prospect to read the letter. What happened was that fans did read the letter attached to the chicken and a $12,000 rubber-chicken campaign generated about $2.5 million in extra renewals.

17

You Can't Do It? That's the Wrong Way to Think!

IT'S TIME FOR a pep talk, you and me. Ready? You're not going to want to hear this, but I'm going to tell you anyway. Here we go.

You can do it.

Yes, you can.

Do yourself a favor. Remove the *can't* from your vocabulary right now, because if you don't, you're going to have an awful time finding success in your life, in business, and especially on the Web. Period. End of story. So unless you're telling me you want to be unsuccessful, then you must listen to my advice and digest it and then live it. Really live it. It can't be faked.

You have to change the way you think. Far too many people go through life with a negative *can't* attitude and because of it, they never accomplish much of anything, let alone anything remarkable.

I know you don't want to be that person.

Not convinced? Maybe you'd like to hear some stories from some people who beat the odds (physical and otherwise) and removed the word *can't* from their lives. Yes, this is intended to make you feel guilty.

Ludwig van Beethoven was deaf. But he is regarded as one of the greatest composers of all time.

Lance Armstrong had testicular cancer. Then he won the Tour de France five more times.

Franklin Delano Roosevelt had polio. He's also the only U.S. president to serve four terms.

Oprah Winfrey was born in the South in 1954 and though she had a fairly traumatic childhood, she rose up to become a prominent talk show host and businesswoman. Oh yeah, she's also got more money than most small countries.

Christopher Reeve (Superman!) was paralyzed from the neck down. After his accident, he became a film director, started the Christopher Reeve Foundation to fund spinal-cord-repair research, lobbied Congress, and crisscrossed the country on speaking engagements.

J. K. Rowling once lived in an Edinburgh, Scotland apartment that was infested by mice, and was on government-assisted living to boot. Less than 10 years from that moment, she became one of the richest women in the world!

Lucille Ball's mother received a letter from the American Academy of Dramatic Arts saying, "Don't put any more money into this. This girl will never make it."

I could go on and on . . . and I will. What about non-famous people who overcame the odds?

Joe Simpson and Simon Yates were the first to scale the west peak of the Siula Grande in the Peruvian Andes. Simpson fell into a 100-foot crevice and Yates had to leave him. Simpson, the guy who fell, crawled out of the crevice and crawled for three days back to base camp.

Was *can't* in Joe's mind?

Manuel de los Santos is a 25-year-old Dominican Republic native who lost his leg in a car accident. Oh yeah, and he can shoot par on a golf course without the use of a prosthetic leg. When he took up the game (after the accident), he hit 2,000 balls a day to practice. A friend of his said he once saw Manuel practicing out of a sand bunker, came back that afternoon, and saw de los Santos in the exact same bunker, working on his short game like a tour professional.

Two thousand balls a day, with one leg? Nobody can do that? Oh wait. . . .

On a personal note, my high-school guidance counselor told me to not even apply for college because my grades were so poor. Turns out, I just didn't like the format in high school. How do I know? I graduated from the University of Akron with a 3.5 GPA, allowing me to begin a career as a writer and Web professional.

What if I had listened to him? If I had, you wouldn't be reading this book.

Remember this key point. If you want to be remarkable, you have to *do* something remarkable.

Can't isn't going to cut it.

There, we got that out of the way. I feel better . . . you?

P.S. Next time you're about to start a project and you feel yourself about ready to drop the *can't* word, I want you to think about some of the stories you've read here today and then honestly ask yourself if you still can't do it.

Also, be honest with yourself. Is it that you can't do it, or you "don't want to do it because it's hard work"? If you want to be successful, there's going to be hard work involved.

18

What's Your Hook?

ARE YOU MEMORABLE? Well, are you? I once met a guy who had the title of "Sales Weasel" on his business card. I'll never forget that guy. I met another lady once who was, in fact, an actual rocket scientist and had the title to prove it. I'll never forget her.

This book is filled with examples of businesses and brands that have caught the attention of their target audiences and then turned that attention into revenue. One of the most important aspects of getting attention for your business is creating a memorable brand. As an individual, are you more likely to be remembered as Scott Ginsberg, or The Name Tag Guy? What's going to pop into your head at your next meeting, the name Joel Libava or his branded name The Franchise King? You get the idea. Unless your name is memorable, it's forgettable. Below are a few memorable brand names that have taken on a life of their own, allowing them to extend their wings into a brave new world of sales, leads, and publicity.

The Tax Mama, aka Eva Rosenberg, never wanted to have a career in accounting and taxes, it just happened. For more than 20 years, she practiced her skills for large and small companies, learning the ins and outs of tax preparation and international business. Then one day she realized that all of the experience she'd built up was easily teachable to so many people who wanted to be just like her, and know what she knew. That's how the brand Tax Mama was born. She now creates seminars and workshops covering valuable information and shares that information with anyone who will pay for it, and people do. Today, her wildly popular Ask TaxMama newsletter and web site (Tax mama.com) helps millions of people find their way through the maze of tax laws, in print, at seminars, and on radio shows across the country.

The Database Diva, aka Lori Feldman, isn't the type of person that would be considered an extrovert. However, when a friend suggested she rebrand herself as "The Database Diva," she went with it. Feldman's expertise is helping businesses use databases to increase sales, so the name fits. Nevertheless, it wasn't always that way. Her previous company name was Aviva LLC, a name that could mean anything. "I had seen other companies that had a concept title with a few words and you looked at that phrase and knew exactly what they did," said Feldman. "And I couldn't figure out what I was at that point."

Feldman went to lunch with a creative friend, who helped her think about her product offerings, her competitive difference, and her target market. "She suggested about 25 names and The Database Diva was on the list," Feldman says. "It just popped off the page—that's what I do!" Today Feldman reaps the rewards of having a memorable name, despite a few negative comments in between. "I knew by calling myself The Database Diva I might turn some people off, and I did. Still I was shocked the first time it happened. I got an opt-out on my marketing e-mail. She unsubscribed and said, 'I can't stand seeing your name.' I looked in my database and she wasn't a customer, and I just thought, 'move on.'" Indeed.

Following are some other names you may have heard of either from this book or in your other travels. Do a search for each one to see how easy it is to find out who they are by visiting AttentiontheBook.com.

Tip: Not everyone is going to like you, and not everyone is going to buy from you. Focus on the customers who like what you represent and what you have to offer. Leave the negative people for someone else. There's no reason to spend a second worrying about someone who's never, ever, going to buy from you.

- The Franchise King
- Ad Hustler
- Name Tag Guy
- Sticker Giant
- Morning Coach
- Tech Czar
- The Question Mark Guy
- The Coupon Mom
- The Biz Web Coach (I cheated, this one is me)

19

A Few More Things about Good Brand Names . . .

Obviously, the biggest reason to have a strong brand name is that if you do it right, it's memorable, and being memorable means that you're both more easily findable and shareable. When you're driving home from the office listing to the radio, are you more likely to remember the name Eva Rosenberg or the name Tax Mama? When you get home and you're searching for information about that ad you heard today a few hours earlier, are you going to have more luck searching for Eva Rosenberg or Tax Mama? Three months later, when you're in a business meeting and someone brings up the point that we need to hire a tax consultant, are you more likely to remember Eva Rosenberg or Tax Mama?

Trademark It!

Once you have a brand name that you're going to stick with, make sure to get it trademarked. This is the brand identity you're going to build a long-term business around. Without a trademark you run the risk of someone else either stealing your name or infringing upon it. Tip: A good place to start your search for free is at U.S. Government Trademark Electronic Search System (TESS). Visit http://tess2.uspto.gov.

Say What You Do!

This one is pretty obvious, but sometimes you have to have someone say it to you in order for it to really stick. If you are the world's best and most accomplished rubber chicken manufacturer, then is it better to brand yourself as XYZ Chicken, LLC, or The Rubber Chicken Guy? If you are the a lawyer from Ohio who specializes in construction law, are you better served branding yourself as XYZ Law Firm, Inc. or Ohio Construction Lawyer? Here's an additional tip before choosing a brand name: Do a domain name search and see if that domain is available. There's no use in branding yourself with something that you can't own the dot-com of.

Monitor Your Reputation!

The good news is that because you're memorable you're going to get a lot of attention and revenue. The bad news is that more people are going to talk about you, and some of it is going to be negative in nature. There's no reason you should be worried about negative talk; it's going to happen to even the best-loved brands. What you should be worried about is brand thieves. People who want to use your good name to sell their junk products, or tell lies about you. That's why it's important to monitor what is being said about your brand online all the time. Use Google News alerts (http://news.google.com/alerts), or a service like Trackur.com to monitor what people are saying about you.

Apply Alliteration!

Alliteration is a literary or rhetorical stylistic device that consists in repeating the same consonant sound at the beginning of several words in close succession. Database Diva, mentioned above, is a great example of this. Names that use alliteration are often more easily remembered.

Dan Schawbel is the bestselling author of *Me 2.0*, publisher of *Personal Branding Magazine*, and PersonalBranding Blog.com. Below are some of his tips on how you can develop your own powerful, and attention-getting personal brand.

> Personal branding in today's world is how you market yourself to others with the goal of standing out, getting attention, and becoming a valuable resource. Celebrities, such as Paris Hilton, Donald Trump, and Oprah, have built extraordinary personal brands that demand a lot of attention. These days, branding isn't just for the celebrities because now everyone can leverage the power, reach, and accessibility of the Internet to manage their own brand.
>
> Your brand is who you are, what you're passionate about, and what you have expertise in. Successful brands have a meaning, values, and are unique. What do you want to be known for? When someone has a specific need, will your name come to their mind first? I always recommend that you select a niche, which is the easiest and most effective way to stand out. You can't beat Suzi Orman in Google for the search results for "personal finance expert," but you can win if you have a niche off of that such as "personal finance expert in Chicago" or "personal finance expert for college students."
>
> Before you try to get attention for yourself, have a deep understanding of why you want that attention and what you want to do with it. For instance, you might want attention for selling a product or a service or to become better known in your niche, which will open up new opportunities. Regardless of your goals, showing up to bat is half of the game, which means that your brand has to be everywhere your audience is searching.

Turning Your Name into a Brand: Ask Dave Taylor

For more years than he wanted to admit, Dave Taylor spent hours each day answering e-mail from people who had read one of his technical computer books or an article he'd written for one magazine or the other. Not terrible, but it was so often the same question again and again, without any sort of efficiencies of scale. In fact, the more popular Dave became and the more he answered questions, the more questions showed up the next morning. Without a penny of compensation.

When blogging first came onto everyone's proverbial radar screen in mid-2003, Dave immediately saw that the combination of being able to publish questions and answers (Q&A) coupled with the ability of readers to leave questions, clarifications, and updates, was a winner. The question was how to format things and what to call them.

He initially thought about a dry business name like "Computer Answers" or "The Tech Support Spot" or similar, but they didn't strike his fancy. Business friends warned him that a business with his name in it would be hard to sell down the road because of how many other Dave Taylors are there out there. However, he didn't care because he couldn't envision selling his blog. Therefore, with some inspiration from his friend Tim Carter, who runs Ask the Builder, he created "Ask Dave Taylor" and got the domain name askdavetaylor.com.

Now Dave was no longer a person, but a brand. It's that easy.

Dave started, slowly at first, to create content. As traffic and revenue grew, Dave became more focused and started to really research what kind of questions and problems people commonly had and how to help them. Around the same time Facebook and Twitter began gaining widespread popularity, so Dave began using those and other social media tools to build his brand. When Dave first started, Twitter wasn't even a gleam in the developer's eye, and Facebook was for college students and still very much an exclusive club.

Social media, however, is a moving target. We all have to keep learning and experimenting, so Dave experiments with how to hook various platforms together. On Twitter, for example, he's @DaveTaylor, not @AskDaveTaylor (though he did reserve the latter name so someone else wouldn't take it). On Facebook, similarly, he's Dave Taylor, and while he has an Ask Dave Taylor Facebook Group, he never really does anything with it other than document how to work with a group.

The icon on Dave's Twitter account is his cartoon from the Ask Dave Taylor site: visual consistency is important and helpful. In the last few months, he's gotten around to having a "follow me on Twitter" link on his blogs to build his social equity even further.

The latest development in the creation of his brand is an Ask Dave Taylor iPhone application (which you can find in the iTunes App Store, if you're curious). This final piece is all part of that "branding in multiple universes" strategy that's so important for a consistent identity across the Web and social media landscape. The web site advertises the app, the app advertises the site, and both his Twitter and Facebook accounts also link back to the web site. It's not enough—it never is—but one of the key concepts behind success in the social media world is what people like Dave call cross-pollination. However people find you, make sure they can easily move from one world to another and find you throughout.

A great tool for helping you check your brand name in social media space is Usernamecheck.com. It's a free service that will check in all the major social media locations to see if your brand name is available. For domain names, try Instantdomainsearch.com.

Dave's plan is similar to the Jim Kukral plan. Like Dave, I have been blogging at JimKukral.com since 2001. When social media started to get hot, I made sure to go out and reserve my name in all the important places like Twitter (@jimkukral) and Facebook (Facebook.com/jimkukral). Whenever a new, hot, potential social network comes out, I always take a moment to go and create an account just to reserve my brand name. You should do the same.

20

Determination, Diligence, and Discipline

WHO WOULD EVER think you could build a brand with never spending one dime on advertising? It's possible and Tim Carter, the Founder of AsktheBuilder.com, did it. Carter did it using the three Ds: Determination, Diligence, and Discipline.

This story is a long one, but fast forward to today and here's what can happen if you invest the time to build a brand. Imagine 48,000 unique visitors a day to a web site you own. Imagine daily residual advertising revenues that exceed $2,000.00 each day. Imagine not having to work each day, if you want, because you built a web site to run on autopilot. Yes, this is what AsktheBuilder.com is all about and Tim Carter is living proof that working smart and hard can produce an income stream that is like the Energizer Bunny—it just keeps on going.

Carter's success is based on his passion as a custom home-builder and remodeling contractor. He loved working with his hands, but while in his mid-30s, he realized that the constant hard physical labor would eventually maim or kill him. It most certainly would affect his quality of life as he aged. In 1993 at age 41, Carter was selected as one of the Top 50 Remodelers in the United States by *Remodeling* magazine. Carter used this award to launch a weekly self-syndicated newspaper column entitled Ask the Builder that was running in 30 newspapers within nine months. This column is still published each week by about 30 papers across the nation, even though the newspaper industry is on life support.

However, Carter quickly discovered that column writers make no money. His average pay from a paper for the one-time license rights to his columns was less than $8 each week. Carter saw who was making the money—the publishers of the newspapers. They did it by selling ads.

In September 1995, Carter saw the Internet for the first time. He had an instant epiphany, realizing that the Internet would allow the rapid transfer of knowledge to those who had a problem. He likened it at that time to an instant digital library that allowed a person to get data and facts without leaving their home. That was a pretty heady prediction back in 1995! Turns out that Carter was right, as he routinely works from home in his PJs.

Building the Brand

It's very important to realize that as he was blazing this new career path in uncharted territory, Carter didn't really have a brand plan. He was a carpenter who graduated from college with a degree in geology. He never took one business course in his life. You don't have to have an MBA to create a brand. It helps no doubt, but it's not necessary. All Carter had were the three Ds.

The most important factor in the overall success of building the AsktheBuilder.com brand was determination. Carter decided in 1993 that he was going to close down his construction business and devote all of his time to his web site. He took failure off the table. His new information business, Ask the Builder, was going to survive and thrive. He had a series of negative business encounters with three clients in a row, and decided no person would ever do that to him again. By deciding that he was not going back to building, he had only one choice for his wife, three young children, and himself. That choice was move forward at any cost and it worked. Carter decided to write about common problems people had with their homes. He offers solutions to the problems in a language the everyday homeowner can understand. AsktheBuilder.com grosses more than $1,000,000 a year in ad sales and the sale of digital electronic products. The vast amount of that revenue is net profit. You can build a brand if you have a similar passion.

When you do an autopsy on the AsktheBuilder.com brand, you discover rapidly some of the ingredients to the success. He decided to write about problems that would be the same 50 years from now so that his columns would always be relevant. He decided at an early date to avoid product reviews as those columns rapidly become dated. Evergreen content allows a brand to have lasting value.

Building a List

Another key ingredient to the success of the AsktheBuilder .com brand is Carter's newsletter list. Carter has more than 100,000 subscribers to his free weekly newsletter. That's more subscribers than many newspapers and magazines have! What Carter discovered is that the newsletter allows him to extend the AsktheBuilder.com brand into the consciousness of each of his subscribers with minimal effort. Carter gives away helpful information each week in the newsletter to each subscriber. This, in turn, triggers a subliminal response in the head of each subscriber that they owe him something. Carter leverages that obligation into elevating the brand in the subscribers' minds. He can also leverage it into cash when he periodically markets a new or existing product to the list.

Build Quality

Carter also helped build the AsktheBuilder.com brand by con-structing each column, each newsletter, and each photo with nothing but high-quality information. Just as other well-known brands (Mercedes, Rolex, LL Bean, and so on) are known for quality merchandise, Carter decided to make that one of his differentiation characteristics. He knew there were other home-improvement web sites and that there would be more in the future, but that few of them would take the time to offer the best content.

You'll also discover that there's a secret weapon Carter uses to leverage his brand. He tells stories and people love stories. Stories captivate the reader and allow the reader to place their situation in the story. Carter tries to tell a story in each of his columns. Don't ever underestimate the power of storytelling.

Staying on the Cutting Edge

Carter continues to build the AsktheBuilder.com brand by trying to stay in the limelight of all the evolving technology. Carter was one of the first YouTube Partners. He's active on Twitter. He uses powerful technology to send out his newsletter and create autoresponder series that help leverage the AsktheBuilder.com brand. In other words, Carter is not afraid to experiment and he recognizes that he must offer solutions to the different subsets of the population in different ways. People consume brands and content differently. One size doesn't necessarily fit all!

21

Marketing and Sales 101

IN ORDER TO understand how to use attention to drive revenue, we first have to take a step back and understand the basic rules of marketing and sales. Now, perhaps you already think you know how this all works, but maybe you just think you know. There is always more that can be learned, especially when we're talking specifically about a Web environment. Fifteen years of selling on the Web has taught me many rules that have allowed me to generate millions of dollars in revenue for my clients and myself. By understanding these rules, you'll finally be able to get what you want for your own business and for your clients as well.

The very first thing you need to do is understand what you're selling and to whom you're selling it. The first part of that is the first step, of course, and we'll talk about that shortly. The second part, the knowing your target audience part, is just as important. Without a clear understanding of who they are, and more specifically, what they want and what problems they have, you'll never be able to get their attention.

First you need to figure out your unique value proposition (UVP).

What Am I Selling That's Better or Different than My Competitor?

This is called a unique value proposition (UVP). James Connor, who wrote *The Perfection of Marketing*, eloquently called this "The Sales Moment." It's that moment when your potential audience clearly understands why they are going to choose you over someone else. Without a clear UVP you'll never effectively be able to market your products/services, and if you can't do that, no amount of attention is going to matter. You'll be dead in the water wondering why all of your effort isn't working. Remember, you can't put the cart before the horse. Developing a strong UVP is your first step.

Let's pretend you own a business called Sarah's Pizza Shack and your competitor on the corner is Paul's Pasta Parlor. You both sell Italian food, and you both cater to the same neighborhood so you're essentially the same to your target marketing, but in reality, you have differences. What are they? They could be:

- You have a much nicer dining room; the competitor's place is like eating in a diner.
- Your children's menu has favorites like chicken and fries, the competitor doesn't.
- You've been in business for 50 years.
- Your staff is friendly and fun.
- Your pizza has won awards for years.
- Your homemade recipe for sauce was brought over from Italy in 1902 by your grandmother.

In other words, your pizza palace rules, and Paul's Parlor is just a pretender. Those are reasons that your customers will choose you over them (your UVP); if you can effectively communicate those messages to them in the right way (getting their attention will be part of that).

Here is an UVP exercise: create your own UVP. List below all the reasons why you are better than your competition and why your customers choose you.

_____

_____

_____

_____

_____

_____

_____

Now remember, Paul is also reading this book, and he's coming up with the same counter-list to you, and he's going to try and beat you by getting those messages out faster than you are, in a more creative and loud way. However, you're not going to let him. You're going to kick Paul's butt because you are a doer, and remember, doers get what they want!

Another fantastic way to find out what your UVP is is to ask your existing customers. You already have those fans; they are the people who currently use your services or buy your product, so why not ask them why they chose you over someone else?

Here's how to ask your customers. Draft up a message that you can either get to them by phone, e-mail, or "gasp" snail mail. The letter should read something like the following, modifying as you see fit.

> Hi Mr. Robinson,
>
> Hope you are doing well this beautiful fall season here in the Cleveland area. My family has been enjoying the weather. In fact, we've spent more time outside this year than ever before. Unfortunately, a lot of that has been raking leaves.
>
> *(continued)*

(*continued*)

I'm contacting you today because I need your help with something. We've been doing business together for a while now and I'd like to thank you for that. In fact, I'd like make you an offer.

How can I help your business grow? What can I do for you?

There has to be something I can do to help you out. Could we get on the phone some time soon, maybe next week, to discuss it? Perhaps I can refer to you some customers of mine who could use your products or services. You never know.

On another note, I need to ask for some help from you as well. I'd like to discuss why you do business with my firm or me. On our call, perhaps you could share that with me, or maybe even contact me back now with some reasons why.

What I'm doing is trying to understand why my customers choose us over all the competition out there. I'm not looking for a ton of reasons, but I will take whatever you have to offer.

Thank you so much for your time and let's get that call scheduled. Please give me a list of times I could call you.

Sincerely,

Jim Kukral

Company Name Here

Phone

E-mail

There are some notes you will need to add when you're constructing that letter. Make sure to personalize the letter instead of using the "Dear Valued Customer" greeting. Customers can spot that line a mile away, and they'll regard it as a generic letter designed to waste their time and most won't read past it, or even if they do, they'll regard it as spam or junk mail.

In addition, notice that each communication should be personal in nature. A form letter that goes out to everyone can work for you, but a more effective approach is to add some personalization into the script. Adding some personal information about you, your family, someone in the office, or whatever shows this isn't a form letter sent to everyone. I have horrible handwriting, but my wife doesn't. In fact, hers is like a font. When I need to send out important information, I often get my wife to personally write the note out in long hand. It makes the note mean 100 percent more, and always gets compliments from the recipient, which, by the way, makes it more memorable and attention getting.

Sure, it's more work, but wait a minute, aren't we doing something that's really important here? This is business! There's a reason we're doing this. Don't do it willy-nilly. Your customer will see right through it, and the results will be lost.

In the sample letter above you will also notice that we lead with a note about how we can help them first. It's always best to open up a conversation with that message as opposed to you asking for what you want. This builds goodwill between you and your customer, and strengthens your request for your own needs, making your customer actually far more likely to help you. Which, of course, is the goal.

What should happen, what *will* happen, is that:

- Your customer will be pleasantly surprised to hear from you and your offer to help them.
- They will pay attention to your request and give you the information you need.
- You'll build some goodwill from them, which gives them even more reasons to never leave you.

You can also hire an outside person to do this for you, if you believe it would sound better coming from a third-party voice. It's sometimes true that a customer will be more candid with someone not associated with your brand, which may end up in more truthful, and sometimes brutal, answers.

At the same time you're talking to your customers, you should ask your sales staff (if you have one) to generate a list of the things they hear from their customers about why they buy from you, and why they don't. Also ask them to include a list of the biggest objections they get as well as the answers they give to those objections. Your sales team, which could even be your affiliates, are on the front lines of communication about your brand, which means they get the most feedback. It also means they know how to sell your product (hopefully) and because of that, they're going to have insight someone in the corporate office will most likely not have.

The next step is to take all the feedback from your customers and your sales staff, put them up on a board in your conference room, and call your entire staff in. Go over each point and get feedback from each person, especially your sales team. Make a lunch of it, order in and let everyone know you value his or her input.

Take that list from your customers and sales team and try to figure out which points are legitimate and which ones are not. Don't argue with them. That's your ego talking. These are comments from your customers and shouldn't be taken as attacks on you. Set your ego aside and listen to what everyone has to say. Then take that final list and prioritize them from top to bottom on how important they are. This will give you a good idea of what you need to know about how your sales and marketing function together from a brand perspective.

Voila! You now have a list of your unique value propositions. Now you know for a fact why your customer chooses you over your competitors. You will also have learned, perhaps, what you're not doing well enough, and, more importantly, what you're not effectively communicating to prospective clients that are holding back sales.

You may think you know how to sell your product, but until you really know, you're guessing. Chances are you will find out a few things that will make you stand up and say, "Wow, I had no idea this feature was that important" or "It's unbelievable we have sales as strong as we do now because it's obvious we weren't telling our customers what they needed to hear."

That's power. That's sales. That's revenue. That's good!

The Two Reasons People Use the Internet

Once you have your UVP, you're ready to move onto the next step, figuring out their pain points and how you're going to take the pain away.

Tim Carter who owns AsktheBuilder.com once told me that people come to the Internet for two reasons and two reasons only:

1. To have a problem solved.
2. To be entertained.

Think about it. Everything we do online falls under one of those two categories. *Everything!* Let me give you some examples.

You're trying to figure out what to cook for dinner. You have chicken in the freezer, but you don't know how to cook it. Maybe you've wanted to learn how to cook your wife's favorite chicken marsala, but you don't know how.

Where do you go? Online of course! Google probably, and you type in something like "Chicken marsala recipes" or "How to cook chicken marsala?" What you get back is millions of results on how to cook chicken marsala . . . go figure. Problem solved.

Maybe you're looking to find that long-lost grade school friend you haven't spoken to in 30 years. You get on Facebook and track them down. Turns out they now live in Japan while you're still residing in Omaha. Facebook solves that problem for you, and before you know it, you're rekindling a long lost friendship message-by-message from across the world. Problem solved.

Maybe you want to have some fun. You had a long day and you'd like to play some games or relax and watch some videos. You could use the Web to visit Yahoo! Games and play scrabble with friends and family, or head on over to YouTube and watch billions of videos. That's entertainment.

Once you understand those two reasons for why people use the Web, you can begin to understand how to find success. Of course, the real trick is to figure out how to do both at the same time. If you can solve problems for people, *and* entertain them, you've crossed-over into that once in a lifetime killer idea that will surely make you get noticed. Strive for that, okay?

22

It's All about Pain

SOLVING A PROBLEM is really all about taking someone's pain away. We all have pain and as consumers we spend trillions of dollars a year on people and businesses who can take the pain away for us. When our teeth hurt we go to the dentist and, literally, he takes the pain away. When our toilet breaks, we call the plumber and she plunges the problem away. When we need to figure out how to generate sales, leads, and publicity by generating attention, we pick up this book!

Everyone has pain and that's why, if you can figure out how to stop that pain, you can make bags and bags of cash. Now is your opportunity to figure out what pain you can take away from your customers. It doesn't matter what it is that you do, there's someone out there that needs your help.

An accountant takes the pain away from people who don't understand things such as taxes and billing procedures. A car salesperson helps us buy the car that will allow us to have that job that makes us money. Even a business like Ikea helps us get over the pain of having to spend too much money on attractive, yet durable furniture.

Getting the idea? You don't sell what you think you sell. Customers buy from you because of what you can do for them to help them, not because of your logo or web site copy. Once you begin to think in these terms you will begin to prosper, because you'll understand how to assist your customers in giving you their business.

Five-Hour Energy drink doesn't sell you energy. They sell you the ability to get more stuff done so you can make more money. Apple doesn't sell you a computer. They sell you status and productivity.

What do you sell? Again, it's probably not what you think it is.

Take a moment and write down the things that your customers get when they purchase your products or services. Not the direct thing they purchase from you, but the after-effects they get from it. You'll find that list to be drastically different from what you thought it was if you do it right.

By the way, this is why Google wins and leads. They continuously deliver the most relevant solutions to our problems in a fast and simple way. They are in the business of taking your pain away, and they do it well.

If they didn't, we wouldn't use them. The same holds true for your business. Are you thinking like Google?

Your Sales Funnel

A sales funnel, also known as a sales pipeline, is the necessary process every successful business needs to have in place in order to maximize their success effectively. Simply put, you have to have a sales funnel in place if you want to, well, make more sales. The entire reason for having a web site or a blog or a landing page is to get someone to take action. As mentioned previously, that action could be filling out a form for a lead for your sales department, getting a new subscriber to your blog, or just getting someone to buy a product or service. Without a sales funnel in place, you'll never be able to know if what you're doing is working or not. You'll be able to guess, sure, but you'll never really know. That's bad marketing.

In a typical sales funnel the wide end at the top of the funnel includes unqualified prospects—the people who you think might need your product or service, but to whom you've never spoken. At the bottom of the funnel, you have people who have received delivery of your product or service and have paid for it.

It all starts at the top with the new opportunity—everyone who comes into contact with you or your business in any way is a new opportunity. Everyone! This means people who find you through social media profiles, such as Twitter, Facebook, and LinkedIn. This also means anyone else who finds out about you or your brand in any other way, offline or online. What most people don't realize is that once someone is brought into your brand, and made aware of you, they are technically a new opportunity ready to be fed into your sales funnel, if you're doing it right. That's why it's important to think about the interactions you have in this manner, to understand that everyone is a customer. Everyone has the potential to either buy from you, or recommend you to someone else at some point during their interaction with you. Failure to succumb to this truth means that you're leaving potential money and customers on the table.

Each new opportunity you create is fed into the top of the funnel and worked down through the funnel in a variety of ways, usually controlled by both the customer and you. Nowadays it's more difficult to control exactly how the customer wants to interact with you and your funnel, which is why you can't afford to let them slip through by not offering them as many options as possible to interact with your brand or you. That means you have to be everywhere, all the time.

Once a potential new customer, or new opportunity, is inside and at the top of your sales funnel, they decide (and you try to lead them) if they're going to go down the funnel and take action. This process usually involves an initial form of communication with you, and then the customer begins to do some research about who you are and what you do. This is the critical step when most potential customers are lost out of the sales funnel. Why? Because too many businesses focus on talking about what they do, instead of talking about what problems they solve for the customer.

The key to keeping customers in your sales funnel and getting them all the way through to an action is to make sure that you are offering them a path to follow. You've already communicated to them what problems you can solve for them, now lead them to your cash register, take their cash, and move onto the next customer. That's how you do this. Wash, rinse, repeat. Over time, and through refinement, you'll begin to see that your sales funnel will become a never-ending supply of customers, enabling you to never have to worry about where the next customer is coming from ever again. And also help you not to spend all the money on advertising that you used to.

My sales funnel looks like this. At the very top I work constantly, more than 50 percent of my time, to bring in new opportunities using multiple strategies. These include social media (Twitter, Facebook, LinkedIn), and also things like speaking gigs; article writing for offline and online publications; being a guest on podcasts, radio, Internet, and television shows; eBooks I write or take part in; or any other ways I can find to get my brand out in front of as many people as possible. Oh yeah, and writing books like this. Because I work so hard to be out there all over the place, my net for reaching new opportunities is very wide, which allows me to reel more fish into my sales funnel, therefore allowing me to have a never-ending database of leads consistently.

It's important to have both the top and the bottom of your sales funnel worked out. Once you have the top of your sales funnel working to generate you countless new opportunities, you need to make sure you have something at the bottom to sell them. This is your offering; the things you are selling or promoting. Again, your offering could be anything (sales of a product/service, subscriptions, e-mail signups, and so on). In my case, I primarily work to funnel new opportunities into my coaching and consulting businesses, but I also consider e-mail subscriptions and social media connections as part of my return on investment.

The beauty of having an effective sales funnel is that there will be a certain amount of people who will never, ever buy from you. However, once you have them inside your sales funnel you will have a much better chance of having them recommend you to someone else.

23

The Universal Truths of Selling on the Web

YOU ALREADY KNOW the biggest universal truth of selling on the Web: solving problems. Now let's talk about some other universal truths that will continue to help you understand how to find success online. You'll notice that these rules are not totally specific to the Web, but are rules that are pretty much universal in marketing and sales. However, these truths are in fact more important in a Web environment, and are consistent in the way they have helped the Web grow into the behemoth that it is today. One thing is for sure, if you want to harness the power of attention to drive more sales or publicity, then you're going to first need to understand these universal truths of marketing and selling online.

Easy and Simple Wins

Google knows this and now you do as well: easy always wins. Take a moment and picture your web site, your blog, your product or service in your head right now. Now, think of

Google's. Which one is easier? No, you're not a search engine; you're probably a small business owner with a variety of products or services, an entrepreneur with a business idea, or a blogger. However, the comparison remains because regardless of what it is you do, easy will always win.

So keep thinking about your Web business. Is what you're selling easy to buy? By that, I mean, when somebody comes to buy from you, or to simply get information from you—like a phone number or to download a white paper—is it easy to do? On the other hand, are you making it too hard?

Picture Google.com again in your head. It's pretty darn easy, isn't it? There's a logo and a big input box underneath it. You put in what you're looking to find, hit search and, boom, you find it. Easy. Google understands that customers use them for one reason, to have a problem solved; therefore, that's what they deliver, without all the frills that other search portals like AOL or Yahoo! try to offer.

Your opportunity right now is to figure out the main one or two reasons people visit your web site, because despite what you might think, your customers probably have only those one or two things on their mind when they visit you.

If you visit the home page of Orbtiz.com, you're probably there to do one of a few things only. Book a flight, find a car, make a hotel reservation, or possibly all three at once. But honestly, that's pretty much it, right? I would bet that 99 percent of their traffic is trying to do one of those things. The same goes for you and your web site, blog, membership site, or anything you produce online.

What exactly are your customers looking for? You need to find out and find out right now! Check your analytics (I recommend Google Analytics, and it's free at www.Google.com/Analytics) to find out things like the most viewed pages of your web site, as well as the most exited pages too. You may find out that 90 percent of your visitors are focusing on the free white paper download page and ignoring the other pages you thought were important. That's great news! Now, you at least know what your customers want and now you can make it easier for them to get it. You may also find out that a large percentage of your visitors always leave your web site on one specific page, giving you the insight that perhaps they aren't finding what they're looking for, getting frustrated, and surfing away. That's bad.

So what should you do with that knowledge to make things easier for your visitor, and better for your business? If you're getting a lot of traffic to your free white paper download, go ahead and take that download information and make it stand out on your home page. If done right, you'll make it as easy as possible for your visitors to get what they were looking for, you'll see even more downloads, and happier visitors because you didn't make them work so hard.

Now, you may also find out that the page you really wanted your visitors to see is not being viewed enough. This could be the specials page on your e-commerce site, or the packages page on your consulting site, or maybe your customer support contact information page. Whatever it may be, once you know what it is, that page obviously needs to be viewed more, and while you can't force it down your visitors digital throats, you can redesign your page so that it limits the other choices that can distract your visitor.

Simple Wins

Choices are great on a menu, but too many choices on your web site or landing page or even with your products can cause indecision because of confusion, and when you're in the business of trying to make a sale, confusion is the enemy. What's the opposite of confusion? The answer is easy. What's the best way to make things easy? Keep them simple.

Often times we're too focused on giving our customers too much. When you go to the barber, he doesn't give you a menu of haircuts. You sit down, tell him simply what you'd like done, he pulls out his tools and cuts your hair. All usually very quickly and without fuss, which is in fact the reason that most men still prefer to go to a barber. Simple. Now if you were to sit in that same barber's chair and instead he gave you a twenty-question survey about what type of hair style you prefer before he started cutting, you'd not only be annoyed, but most likely not want to go to him anymore.

Let's take a further look at an online example to prove the point. Imagine you're visiting the e-commerce store of your favorite pet supply retailer. You need a new collar for your Labrador named Bella. Upon arriving at the site's dog collar section, you find twenty different types and brands of collars. There are fancy collars, cheap collars, chain collars, collars for small and big dogs, collars with diamond studs on them, fashionable collars, and many more. Whew, you're faced with lots of choices.

"Great," you say. "I love it that this store has so many choices, I came to the right place." However, perhaps it's not so great. Having too many choices might be a problem. You just wanted to get a collar. You were ready to buy one. Now you've found out that there are a lot of decisions you need to make before you buy one. You think to yourself, "I had no idea there were so many collars. I like so many of them; I don't know what to choose."

So you didn't buy anything—you were ready to, but you didn't. Chances are this has happened to you at some point in your buying life, and chances are that what happened was you were ready to decide, but the explosion of choices either confused you, or made you realize that you weren't ready to decide. Effective sales and marketing is all about helping the customer make a decision and simplicity is necessary to make that happen.

Examples of making it too hard are:

- Poor navigation so your customer has to figure out where to go.
- A poor unique value proposition (UVP).
- Too many choices of products and services and not being clear about which one is the right choice for the customer.
- Tons of drawn out copy that nobody wants to read.
- Requiring a customer to register before they can buy from you.

People Love Discounts (Everyone's a Shopper)

There's a reason why so many retailers offer coupons and discounts. It's because they work. Even before the dawn of the Internet and the proliferation of choices that came with it, shoppers tended to make purchasing decisions more often when they felt they were getting a deal. Now, with the prevalence of the Internet, it is easier for shoppers to find those deals, from you or from your competitors. Therefore, you should offer it to them if you want more of their business. Everything you sell should show some type of discount on it, or at least the perception of a deal. If you're selling a subscription to your monthly newsletter for $12.00 a month, then why not offer a discounted yearly subscription fee at 30 percent off? Be sure to show the exact amount of value the customer is receiving. For example, order for the year and get 30 percent off the normal subscription fee. That's a value and savings of $30. Magazines have used this technique forever, because it works.

Coupons are another helpful way to get more customers. Many businesses don't think they can use coupons because they feel it cheapens them in the eyes of the customer. This can be true in some cases; however, if done correctly it can work like a charm. The trick is to offer coupons in a classy way, not like something you cut out of the Sunday paper. A coupon doesn't have to be like that. A coupon can be something you can casually place inside an e-mail newsletter that offers a discount for all new orders in the next 30 days. A coupon could be a direct mail postcard that the customer could use to go online and get a special price.

Free Rules

Everyone loves free, especially on the Internet. Craigslist is free, always has been, and has blossomed into one of the biggest online marketplaces, effectively killing off traditional paid classified ads in the process. eBay is free, for the buyer that is. The seller has to pay a fee to post a listing. It's free to watch, and upload millions upon millions of videos on YouTube and other places like Hulu. You can listen to music all day long for free on Pandora.com, assuming you're okay with the ads.

Noticing a trend here? The biggest, best, and most popular sites on the Web are free. The truth is that free is a powerful lead generator and traffic generator. If you can offer some type of free something, anything of value, then you're going to find that you get more traffic and leads into your sales funnel. The challenge for you is to figure out how. Of course, you don't want to go and give away everything you offer for free, but maybe there's a certain selection of things you have that you can give away for free to use as lead generators. For example:

- Are you a blogger? Maybe you have a collection of previously recorded podcasts sitting around that you can give away in order to entice someone to join your e-mail list. If not, make some, c'mon!
- Are you a consultant? Maybe you can offer a free hour of your time to a customer who just needs some questions answered. You do realize that if you can get a potential customer on the phone or in person you have a *much* greater chance of closing them as a customer, right?
- Do you know a lot about something? Maybe you can hold a Webinar where you can teach potential customers what you know. Then maybe you could hold that same event locally in-person?
- Are you a recruiter of jobs? Maybe you could create a guidebook or course that potential employees could use to improve their careers. Let potential job seekers join your e-mail list to get the free guide, then use those contacts as your pool of recruits.

The point is that you need to start thinking about free and the potential it has to bring in more leads and attention for your business or brand.

Make It Simple for People to Buy from You

If you've done your job right, and you've got a customer standing in front of you with cash in hand, then you've got to make sure you are able to take that cash and put it in your pocket. However, too many businesses make it too difficult for their customers to buy from them. Consultants and service businesses screw this up all the time. They build pages and pages of content about what they can do for their customers, yet when the customer is ready to buy, they're asked to "call for a quote" or "contact us to get started." Or worse yet, the dreaded PayPal button. Here's a tip. Most people (your customers) don't get PayPal. They don't know what it is. They don't think it's secure and most importantly, they don't keep money sitting around inside of it. Sure, you can enter a credit card into PayPal, but you still have to go through the PayPal interface. You want to make it truly easy for someone to give you their money online? Get a merchant account and process credit cards the way everyone is used to doing it.

Why are you making it so hard for someone to give you their money? Asking someone to "call for a quote" is like saying, "we need to find out how much money you have first, and then we'll give you a price." At least that's what the customer is thinking. Every business, regardless of what you offer, should and can have some type of packages or set pricing in place for people who want it. If not, you're leaving a large percentage of cashola on the table that they were ready to hand over to you.

Graphic designers are usually the worst offenders at this. They say, "We can quote you as soon as you tell us exactly what you want." Fine, I get it, but not everyone wants to play that game anymore. Why not instead offer a few packages that a customer can evaluate, and buy, without having to interact with you first. It's easier than it looks. Here's an example:

- *Package A: New Business Logo/Branding Package—$499*
  This package is perfect for the new business or brand who wants to get a professional logo that will make them stand out! You get five different logo concepts to choose from, as

well as up to three revisions. Final logo is delivered in digital format as a vector image allowing you to use it on business cards, web sites, brochures, and anywhere you need it. If you order by September 2010, you get 20 percent off! Click the order now button below to get started.

- *Package B: Rebranding Logo/Branding Package—$1,499*
  This package is perfect for the business or brand who needs to rebrand themselves. You get twenty-five different logo concepts to choose from, as well as up to ten revisions. Final logo is delivered in digital format as a vector image allowing you to use it on business cards, web sites, brochures, and anywhere you need it. If you order by September 2010, you get 20 percent off! Click the order now button below to get started.

Tell me, if posed with those choices or "call me for a quote," which one are you more likely to choose? The point is that there are going to be a large percentage of your customers who won't need, or want, to "contact you for more information." They will simply see the package they want and click to buy it.

In order for this to work, you have to make sure you have a secure, safe way for the customer to pay you right then and there. As mentioned a minute ago, you should consider getting a merchant account so you can accept credit cards. Sure, it's a pain in the butt to set up, and those annoying fees from the card companies stink, but it's the cost of doing business on the Web. If you don't want to spring for a merchant account and offer credit card transactions right away, then ok, at the very least use a PayPal buy button. However, again, many customers aren't going to want to use PayPal. Small businesses owners or employees at corporations don't have access to PayPal accounts. However, many of them do have corporate credit cards. Again, make it easy for them.

You may be saying to yourself that your business is different, that you can't offer packages. Bullcrap! The truth is you don't want to, either because it's not how you've done business forever, or you just don't like the taste of it. Fine, but know this though, the days are gone when a potential customer had only a few choices. Sure, it used to be only you and your competitor, but now your customer has more options. They're often going to choose the company that makes it easier for them. You know this is true. You do the same thing when you go shopping for anything. Deny this at your own peril.

PART

24

Making Money on the Web

WE ALL WANT to know how to make more money and work less (or not at all). We dream of the day when we can tell our boss to shove it and spend our time lounging by the pool or traveling the world first-class. We look around at the successful people driving their fancy cars and living in their big mansions and wonder to ourselves, "How can I be like them?" We equate financial freedom with happiness, so we spend our lives in pursuit of that dream.

If we only had more money, everything would just be easier and we'd be happier and stress free, right? If we owned the company instead of working at it, we'd work less and be richer, right? If we didn't have to worry about paying for health care for our family, we'd quit this job we hate, right?

It all sounds so familiar doesn't it? Sure it does, because you're not in the secret society of people who have learned how to create the life of their dreams by using the Internet . . . yet. That's right, yet.

Here's the good news:

- There's never been a greater time in the history of the world to create a business and promote it for virtually nothing.
- This section is going to outline everything you need to know about how this secret society makes money online.

Ok, now here's the bad news:

- It's a lot of hard work.
- You will fail, if you don't try.

However, you're not going to fail! How do I know? I know because you picked up this book. Additionally because you realize that if you're ever going to live the life of your dreams you're going to have to take the chance and make the effort necessary to succeed. So let's start with a little motivation to get you going, then we'll talk about the methods and tools you can utilize to join that secret society of Web millionaires.

25

Do People Really Make Millions Online?

PROBABLY ONE OF the biggest misconceptions about successful people on the Web is that they are all spammers or scammers who make their money from selling porn, advertising bad info-products, or sending spam e-mail messages. Sure, there's a large contingent of those types of people who do profit by the millions by using those tactics, and yes, they *do* make a lot of money. However, what most people don't realize is that there's a completely different set of Web millionaires who do it legitimately operating as regular businesses or individuals. This book will only focus on those people: The real business people who are no different from the attorney or plumber in your neighborhood who work tirelessly and face the same challenges as every business does. The exception being that they do it online.

One of the biggest lures of making money online is that anyone can do it, without having to have a million-dollar marketing budget or team of employees. Yes, you, who has the full-time job. You can begin to build a Web empire in your spare time after you put the kids to bed and before your head hits the pillow each night. Yes, you, the small-business owner who is struggling to make ends meet and realizes that if you could move some or all of your business onto the Web you'd lower costs and profit more.

Believe that it's entirely possible for *you* to do it, if you're willing to put in the effort to go out there to try and learn, with a high emphasis on the *try* part. Remember, doers get what they want, and everyone else gets what they get.

To be one of those doers, you sometimes need a bit of motivation to get you going. Here are a few lessons I've learned from having worked on the Web for over 15 years.

Lesson #1: Doubt Kills Success

One of the main reasons why people aren't doers is because they have doubt. They ask themselves questions like, "Will this work?" or "Can I really do it?" They might even worry that people might laugh at them. Then they get stuck in the details of the strategy and lose focus. They ask themselves, "Am I setting this up the right way?" or "Do I have the pricing right?" These are all legitimate questions we all face when trying something new like starting an Internet business.

When you cannot let go of your doubt, it can stop you from moving forward in the right direction. Doubt kills success. It stops you from taking chances. It hinders you from making important decisions that need to be made. It slows down progress. To be successful online, you have to find a way to push your doubt aside and move forward. Follow your passion and beliefs and do something!

The best way to kill doubt is to focus on your objective, create a plan, and stick to it. Write down your goals on a piece of paper and set deadlines. At some point you *will* question those deadlines because of doubt, but continue to push through and make them happen. Remember, one of the best parts about doing business on the Web is that nothing is set in stone. The Web offers us the ability to constantly update and change our plans and objectives.

Lesson #2: Get Productive or Perish

Distractions kill productivity and if you're not being productive, you're falling behind. One of the downsides of living in a connected world is that we are more accessible than ever before. We are never without our cell phones and our e-mail rarely goes unchecked for long. Facebook, Twitter, and social media in general have made us even more accessible. We're constantly checking in on what our friends and associates are doing and spending precious productive time posting our own updates back out to the world about what we're doing.

To be successful online you must learn how to stop being distracted. Easier said than done, I know. I can tell you from experience, however, that if you can come up with a way to do it you can get more done. For example, right now, as I am writing this book, I have purposely shut off my cell phone and closed my Gmail. I have also turned off my Tweetdeck (the program I use to monitor Twitter) so that I'm not distracted by the daily and never-ending stream of virtual consciousness. However, that's not all, I have also decided that I am not allowed to check my Gmail or Twitter until 3 hours from when I begin writing. This is my own self-appointed deadline to ensure I stay focused on writing.

Another way to help productivity is to set deadlines and create schedules for yourself. Before you go home for the evening, write down a list of the things you want to accomplish the next day. Then when you come in the next day, you know that you have those things to get done, and chances are, if you set a deadline, they will get done. One way to ensure they get done is to promise yourself a reward for meeting a deadline. Perhaps you can promise yourself that if you meet your noon deadline you can treat yourself to a nice lunch out that day. Maybe you can reward yourself by saying if I meet all of my goals by this day, I can take the next day off.

Lesson #3: Be Extraordinary and Remarkable

It's easy to be jealous of successful people. You know, the people who have way more money than you do, or who own many successful businesses, or who have become famous. Are you somebody who thinks, "These people suck because I'm not them." or "Why can't I be like them?"

Well, you can. However, you first have to realize that nobody handed it to them. Remarkable people are remarkable because they've done something remarkable. They didn't wake up one day and were handed fame and fortune and neither will you. Until you understand that you are going to have to go out there and actually do something extraordinary to be extraordinary, you're going to have a hard time finding the success you wish to achieve, on or off the Web.

One of the best ways to gain insight and inspiration is to spend time around remarkable people. You quickly realize that there's no such thing as overnight success. Take Chris Brogan (www.ChrisBrogan.com). Talk about a guy who makes it look super easy, yet, if you spend any time with him you'll see that he works his butt off. In the excellent "Overnight Success" series on his blog, Chris says, "Overnight success doesn't sleep in. Overnight success doesn't watch a lot of TV. Overnight success doesn't have a lot of hobbies right now." He's right. Every single successful person I know got there because they work ten times harder than everyone else does.

There's no such thing as an overnight success, except for lottery winners or people born into the lucky sperm club. You will do better when you lose the jealousy and realize that if you want to be someone like Chris Brogan, you're going to have to work hard just like him. Don't forget it's more than just working hard. You're going to have to do something better and possibly different as well.

One last time: Remarkable people are remarkable because they've done something remarkable. What have you done? Get to work.

Lesson #4: Doers Get What They Want, Everyone Else Gets What They Get

You have questions like, "How do I make myself more memorable? How do I get a better career? How do I make more money so I can quit my job? How do I become successful?"

The answer is that nobody is going to hand all of that to you if that's what you thought. The Internet rewards those who make things happen and try, test, and build. You don't get in shape by sitting on the couch. You don't learn how to speak Japanese by watching old samurai movies. Get off your butt and make something happen.

Lesson #5: Are You a Loser or a Failure?

Losers quit. Failures get back up and try again. On the Web, the people who succeed the most are those who take chances and who aren't afraid to fail. Don't let the fear of failure stop you from trying, and don't let anyone tell you you're a loser. A loser is someone who's afraid to try again after failing.

Lesson #6: Negativity Kills

Probably one of the hardest things about participating in the online world is the transparency involved in it. When you put yourself out there for all to see, you open yourself up to a lot of criticism and negativity. Negative people revel in the anonymity and impersonal communication the Web brings us, through blog comments, forums, and e-mails. They lash out in ways they never would in a face-to-face meeting. They try to bring you and your ideas down either because they didn't think of them first, because of jealousy or, heck, just because they're nasty people. Your challenge is to develop a thick skin. People will say nasty things about you and your business, and it will be up to you to decide how to handle it. The smart play is to kill them with kindness. Resist the urge to ignore them, instead diffuse them inch by inch, with a smile.

All that being said, let me show you the ways that successful people build businesses and brands on the Web and make a lot of money. You can use these business models to create your own special path to success.

26

So How Do People Make Money Online?

THERE ARE A lot of different paths you can go down when planning a successful Web business or strategy. The trick is to figure out which one is right for you and your specific situation. However, before you pick the one that is right for you, it's important to take a step back and define your short- and long-term goals, otherwise, you may find yourself spending years of time working on something that could be a big waste of your time.

Everyone has different goals when it comes to building a Web business, and those goals can be divided into short- and long-term goals. For example, you may simply be interested in earning enough money online to be able to quit your job. That's a great short-term goal. However, perhaps the long-term goal is to be able to take the business you build and sell it off someday.

Short-Term Goals to Get Started

Let's consider the scenario that you want to build a Web business that earns enough revenue on a consistent basis that you can quit your job and work for yourself. The very first thing to do is to figure out what it is that you are passionate and knowledgeable about. The truth is . . .

Everyone Knows a Lot about Something

Darren Rowse, otherwise known as Problogger.net, slowly and quietly built a million-dollar brand for himself on the Web by becoming the world's authority on how to create and profit from a blog. How did he do it? It all started with a domain name and a passion for blogging, which he then built up over time as THE most trusted and respected resource in the world of professional blogging, all from his living room in Australia. Rowse realized that he knew a lot about the business of blogging early, so he took that knowledge and used it to help educate millions of others with a craving for that information.

Brian Clark, also known as Copyblogger.com, spent 2 years giving away free information about how to write powerful and profitable copy for the Web. In return, Clark, a former lawyer with a knack for words, now holds the title as one of the most influential and skilled copywriters online. This influence has allowed him to launch a litany of profitable products which his eager readers snatch up without question.

Joel Libava took his years of experience and expertise as a franchise owner and turned it into a well-known brand and business called The Franchise King. Libava leveraged his knowledge into a successful franchise coaching business. He is also a frequent media personality having become a trusted resource for newspapers, magazines, TV stations, and radio stations all over the country.

Shawn Collins and Missy Ward took their years of knowledge and experience in affiliate marketing and created the world's largest affiliate marketing conference and industry mega-brand called the Affiliate Summit.

The above are only a few examples of regular people taking the knowledge that they have in their heads, and transferring it to the Web. Millions of people just like Darren, Brian, Joel, Shawn, and Missy wake up every day and reach for Internet millions using the same philosophy, and so can you. You simply have to figure out what it is you know a lot about, or are really good at.

Here's an exercise for you: Get out a piece of paper or open a Word document and write down a list of subjects you happen to know a lot about. It can be anything. Maybe you're the world's best stay-at-home mom, or you happen to be really good at playing World of Warcraft. It doesn't matter how silly or small or weird you think it is, and here's why: The truth is that, whatever you happen to know a lot about or are really good at, there are people out there who want to know what you know. That's the truth. It's the reason why Google makes billions of dollars and why the Internet spins around and around. People want to find answers to their problems. Like Google, you're going to give it to them.

So what's on that list you just made? You did make the list, didn't you? Here's some space for you to write them down. Nobody is going to hold you to this list. Just do it! Remember that your list should only include the things you have some passion about. There's no need to build a life/business plan around something you're not going to want to do a year from now.

_____

_____

_____

_____

_____

_____

_____

_____

_____

Don't look now, but you just created the basis for building a product or service that can generate revenue for the rest of your life. This is a *major step!* One of these is your new signature product. People spend their entire lives never narrowing down their passions and expertise into a list like this. Frankly, that's why they continue to work for other people in jobs they hate and industries they have no passion for. You're on your way!

Take a closer look at your list and think about how what you wrote down can solve problems for other people. For example, maybe you wrote down that you are a fantastic organic chef. Think about why someone would want to either hire you or want to know what you know. It takes a few tries to get it right, so don't worry. Here are a few examples:

- *What I know a lot about or am really good at: Organic cooking.*
  What problems I solve for other people: (1) People want to eat and cook healthier and I can give them recipes to do that. (2) People need to hire me to cook or cater for them. (3) People want me to teach them what I know so they can become like me.

- *What I know a lot about or am really good at: Martial arts.*
  What problems I solve for other people: (1) People want to learn how to protect themselves, so they want me to teach them. (2) People want to know how I became an expert so they want me to teach them so they can do it too. (3) People want to kick some butt! I can show them how. (4) People want to get healthier and in shape and my training will help them do that.

  See how this works? What you do, or what you know a lot about, is valuable to other people. You can create revenue by building a product or service that helps people solve their problems. Let's do one more just to make sure you get it. Let's say you're really good at finding deals and coupons online.

- *What I know a lot about or am really good at: Finding Web deals and coupons.*
  What problems I solve for other people: People want to save money and I can show them how and where to do it on the Web.

Do you see? You have something other people want and if you package it right you can make money along the way. The key is to understand that everyone has pain. If you can remove their pain, you will find that not only will they pay you for it, they'll also love you in the process. Think about all the great products and services you use in your everyday life that take away pain and how you revere the ones that do it the best and take away the most pain. That's what you want to do.

27

What's Your $$$ Number?

EVERYONE HAS—OR SHOULD have—a figure in their head that they would need to earn. This is the amount of dollars you need to make every month to be comfortable, feed your family, and pay all of your bills. Don't come up with an inflated number at this point, just a realistic one. I mean really, of course, you want a Ferrari, but is that a realistic goal for this exercise? The answer is no. Instead, base this number off of your needs. For example, you have it figured that you need to earn $10,000 per month to be able to pay all of your bills and take your family on vacation every year. That's a good number, although, it could be lower or higher. It's really up to you. For this exercise, you need to have it in your head or write it down. Got it?

Write it down here if you want: I need to make $_____ per month.

Let's say, for example, your number is $10,000 per month—great. Apply that number to your list of things you know a lot about and you now have the very basic elements of your short-term plan for making money online. Now it's time to figure out how you're going to get there. That's where all of the strategies and methodologies of making money online will come in. You're going to need to choose which subject, or subjects, makes the most sense for you based upon your goals. It sounds easier than it looks, but bear with me. Once we go over all of the different ways you can turn your expertise into revenue you'll have a clearer idea of where to go and what to do.

Still with me? We're about to get into the specific methods you can utilize to generate revenue online. We'll cover them in detail, with examples. If you already have an existing business, you may feel the urge to skip over the following information, but don't. Inevitably, there is always some little tidbit of knowledge or nugget of information that you will gain from brushing up on the things you already know about.

28

Membership Web Sites and Recurring Revenue, Oh My!

HOW WOULD YOU like to make money from the same customer not once, not twice, but over and over and over again? Smart businesses understand that this model is a much better way to feed their balance sheets and keep the budgets overflowing. The idea is to get a customer to give them money on a recurring basis rather than just once. This is called continuity or recurring revenue and is practiced on the Web in the form of a membership program.

The reason membership programs are so valuable is that they can replace your salary by giving you an almost guaranteed stream of revenue month to month, and frankly, if you're going to quit your job to start an online business, you want to ensure you have that recurring revenue. If you've ever worked on the financial aspects of a business, or worked with a venture capitalist, you know that recurring revenue is one of the most important objectives to achieve. It's simple. Your business is *much* more valuable to you and to potential investors if you can show consistent revenue over time, hopefully on an upward scale.

Fact: It's much better to have a customer pay you over and over as opposed to only once. That's why so many Web entrepreneurs and regular offline businesses have begun to implement membership programs. It's also exactly the reason why you need to do it, and do it soon. To give you an idea of what types of membership programs you could create, let's look at a bunch of successful programs and analyze why they work and talk about their earning potential.

Aaron Wall was already the number one do-it-yourself search engine optimization (SEO) resource on the Internet when his wife convinced him to take it up a notch and offer a monthly member training program at SEObook.com. From his web site:

> Launched in 2003, we have one of the oldest standing SEO sites that is still regularly updated. The site originally was designed as a blog that offered DIY [do-it-yourself] SEO tips and helped sell the leading SEO ebook, which had sold well over $1,000,000 in volume. My wife Giovanna found me by being a customer of my ebook. After having been scammed by a shoddy SEO firm for over $5,000, she saw that my $79 ebook delivered far more value than what other people were charging many thousands of dollars for. In 2006, we hit it off, she started ranking #1 for her most valuable keyword, and she pushed me to build an online training program to help other small businesses compete online.
>
> The SEObook online training program initially launched at a price point of $100 a month and has since been raised to $300 a month. So what do you get for that monthly fee? Our ebook customers kept wanting more interaction with us, but we needed a way to facilitate the additional interaction. We stopped taking on many new traditional SEO clients, and shifted toward building the #1 online SEO training program consisting of:

- over 100 custom training modules.
- a private support community that is simply unmatched by any other SEO conference or SEO forum.
- exclusive premium tools.
- monthly newsletters, member's only videos, process flow-charts, custom SEO spreadsheets, and more.

That's quite a bit of information for a low monthly fee, wouldn't you say? As you can see with Aaron's program, if you want to charge premium prices, you're going to need to deliver significant value in return. SEObook offers more than a bunch of articles about how to do SEO. Anyone can go online and find that information on their own. Instead, it offers access to a vibrant community, training modules, and premium tools.

Nobody knows for sure exactly how many members are in the SEObook.com training program, and Aaron isn't ready to say just now, but let's run a few numbers to see how profitable something like this can be.

Let's say that he consistently has 1,000 subscribers each month. 1,000 members x $300 = $300,000 a month, or a yearly revenue total of $3,600,000. Heck, even half of that number is $150,000 a month, SEObook would then bring in $1,800,000 a year. How would you like to bring in a paycheck like that? Of course you would, and it's entirely possible. The best part is it doesn't have to be done by hiring 100 employees. In theory, you could run a program like this with a skeleton crew of employees and virtual assistants.

What you will also find out when running a membership program is that a lot of people choose the "set it and forget it" plan. Those people will join your program, log in once, or maybe never, and still continue to pay your monthly fee over and over. Some continuity experts suggest this can be anywhere from 5–15 percent of your members. That's a whole lotta revenue pouring into your wallet every month for doing nothing. The "set it and forget it" people seem to think that the concept of just buying access to the program will magically help them find success, or lose weight, or stop smoking or, well, you get the idea. What happens is that they join the member program and then they figure out that you actually have to do some work to be successful. I suppose they were expecting an easy button, right? *That's exactly what people are looking for, remember that.*

So once they figure out that accomplishing their goal has more work involved than they anticipated, they become disenchanted with the concept, and either continue the membership in the hopes that they will one day use it, or are too embarrassed to quit or unsubscribe to the member program because it would then admit failure on their part. Ah, the human brain really works in mysterious ways, doesn't it?

You can create a member program for just about anything. If you're a software company, you can let consumers subscribe to use your service. On the Web, this can mean a goldmine, assuming you have a product or service that actually helps people and provides value beyond the one-time purchase and need. Below are a few examples of Web-based software member programs:

Companies like Prfessor.com offer consumers the ability to create their very own online university, academy, or training center for only $49.97 a month. Wordtracker.com offers businesses the ability to do keyword research for the most searched for words and phrases online allowing them to shoot for higher search engine rankings, all for $59.00 a month.

Ever use Netflix.com? Netflix revolutionized the movie rental business by understanding that people didn't really enjoy having to get in the car to go rent a video. Wouldn't it just be easier if the videos were delivered to me? For the small monthly fee of $8.99, Netflix will allow you to pick a movie out online and have it delivered to your home via regular U.S. mail. Then, when you're done, you ship it back via mail and get another one. How can they make money at such a low price point? One million subscribers at the $8.99 monthly price point will bring in $8.9 million a month alone, and the $8.99 price point is only their lowest package. The best part is they have no retail stores, which means no rent or unhappy teenage employees to deal with.

Even Microsoft gets into the continuity action through their Xbox LIVE product. For $7.95 a month, millions of gamers have the opportunity to be entertained by connecting with each other to play games together or add game add-ons like new songs, levels, and characters. The power of the community is what really drives this program. You're most likely not paying $7.95 a month because you want some extra add-ons. You're paying $7.95 a month to be entertained and connected with a vibrant community of like-minded gamers just like you.

Zappos is the king of customer service and one of the true e-commerce beasts on the Web. I once visited their offices in Las Vegas for a tour and was shown their daily sales numbers, which averaged about $3 to $4 million per day. These people know how to make money online; in fact, they're on track now to do a billion dollars a year regularly. They also know how to build a brand and do excellent customer service, having been written up in countless publications and books for years now as *the* example of how to do things right. All that good press has paid off in not only e-commerce sales of products, but also in other ways.

Since their brand and the Zappos way have become legendary in the media, they have elevated themselves to rock star status, which means they had major demand from other businesses wanting to know how they did it. Therefore, they created a program called Zappos Insights, a subscription video service that lets companies ask questions about the Zappos way and get answers from actual Zappos employees. The fee to subscribe every month is $39.95. The service, said CEO Tony Hsieh, is targeted at the Fortune One Million looking to build their businesses. "There are management consulting firms that charge really high rates," Hsieh said. "We wanted to come up with something that's accessible to almost any business."

How many other businesses do you think want to learn how Zappos makes a billion dollars a year: one-hundred thousand, one million, ten million? All of them! Now, if you're one of those businesses, are you going to balk at spending $39.95 a month for the possibility of learning how? Of course you're not; it's a no-brainer.

Maybe you'd like to get started by adding a continuity program on top of your existing business, which will add a continuous stream of income that will make your CFO do back flips. No problem. The first thing you need to do is decide what type of continuity program to put in place and then how to get it done. The next several chapters will show you some options.

29

CD or DVD Continuity Programs

CD OR DVD continuity programs work because people like receiving something in the mail. Something they can hold in their hands, touch, feel, and use. Many businesses don't reach their maximum potential because they fail to realize this fact. People will often pay more, and more often, for tangible things. Information products are great, and require less overhead, but at the end of the day, the consumer usually goes for something they can touch and feel and receive in the mail. That's why CD or DVD programs work so well.

The DVD or CD doesn't have to be the main product you sell. It could be a bonus item included for the customer. For example, if you're offering customers monthly podcast interviews from famous people in your industry, you could offer those for viewing online, and then also, as a bonus, throw the audio file on a DVD and send it out to their physical location. Now you're saying to yourself, "How am I going to do that? Sounds pricey and hard to do?" It's neither of them. At first, you can do it yourself. Head on over to your local office store and grab some cheap CDs or DVDs and some cases. Manually copy the audio file, or whatever it is you're providing, onto the disc, drop it in a case, and throw it in the mail. Later on when you have so many to send that it's overwhelming, use a disc copy service to do it for you. These companies can operate as a complete fulfillment house as well, taking care of sending your discs out for you too. Contact me if you want a referral to a few companies that can help you accomplish this.

You don't have to use DVDs or CDs. Memory sticks are another great option for you. Alternatively, you can even produce a printed publication like a newsletter or magazine.

30

Boot Camps and Training Sessions

ANOTHER GREAT WAY to offer continuity programs is by offering the program over a specific time period in the form of a boot camp or training session. For example, you could create a boot camp event on any topic, and then deliver the content each week in the form of Webinars, teleseminars, group calls, or prewritten e-mails. Whatever, it doesn't really matter how you deliver it, only that you ensure the customer gets it on a consistent basis as you promised.

I run a successful boot camp at 5DayBootcamp.com where I have helped thousands of people learn how to get motivated to find success on the Web. The user signs up to join my e-mail list, and then every day, for the next 5 days, I deliver to them a motivational podcast via e-mail, all automated. My boot camp is free, but I could have easily charged a fee for it. I use it to generate leads for my consulting business, but more on that later.

It doesn't have to be called a boot camp. You can call it a training session or course. The point is you deliver some type of information to the customer on a preset schedule that is determined by you. Think about all of the things you know a lot about or are really good at doing. Simply take that skill, or that knowledge, and break it up into a scheduled training course. Boot camps, training sessions, and courses work because people are used to learning on a schedule. Our educational systems are built on this structure.

To increase your chances of being successful, don't just fill your content up with a bunch of articles. To really make the most value create videos that show people how to do what it is they are paying you to learn about doing. Anyone can go online and find millions of web sites, articles, and blog posts to read, but does that information exist in video form? Probably not. You can be the first to do that, and when you're first, you usually win. The question for you is: are you going to win or let your competitor win?

31

Group Coaching

In 2008, THE recession hit the United States very hard. Jobs were being lost at a record pace, and, in general, the economy was seeing some of its worst moments since the Great Depression. However, on the flip side, the coaching industry went through the roof! Why did this happen? Because so many people who had lost their jobs became accidental entrepreneurs.

Business and Web coaches began to appear, all offering these new customers the resources needed to achieve their own life or business goals. Personally, I launched a business called TheBiz WebCoach.com in 2008 and had an amazingly successful first year helping thousands of aspiring entrepreneurs create their own Web businesses.

You can do it as well. If you have knowledge that can help other people, some skill or success plan that people need to have, then you can turn that into a group-coaching program. The concept is pretty simple. You find people who need what you are offering, have them subscribe to your program, and coach them as a group. You do it as a group for a few reasons:

1. It's much easier to coach a group. Setup a conference call line and let the group members call in once a week during a preset time to speak to you.
2. It's less time consuming. One-on-one coaching is great and profitable, but takes a lot of time.
3. You make more money. Imagine having 500 group members paying you $50 a month. That's what we're talking about here; big money for less work.

One of the big disadvantages to a group-coaching program is that you can't spend one-on-one time with your customers. However, because you are not charging a gigantic monthly fee the customer is presold to be okay with not having one-on-one time. You can always offer them a special one-on-one offer at a special higher price if that's what they need. In fact, always make sure to do that. There is always a certain percentage of your customer base that will opt for the private program. Just don't sell too many of them or you'll be spending all of your time servicing them instead of going for the high-volume group program that requires less time and effort.

Your goal is to work less and make more money, plain and simple. If you want to work more hours, then good for you, but I'm guessing that you don't want that. A group coaching program, setup the right way, will allow you to coach a higher quantity of people at the same time allowing you to earn a lot more revenue.

32

Keeping Subscribers

ONCE YOU HAVE a steady base of subscribers in your program, the trick now is to keep them. This is why you must continuously provide value, month after month. Your customer will stick with you if you do that. The following are some other tips to keep subscribers.

Love Your Members

Once you have a subscriber, you should make that subscriber feel special. Offer your subscribers members-only products and services that truly show your appreciation. Go above and beyond what you normally do. Then watch as they never, ever leave you.

Community

One of the best things you can offer your subscriber base is access to a vibrant community. Create a mastermind e-mail group or private message board area where your members can interact and help each other. This helps take some of the pressure off you as the only content provider and answer person, as well as helps your members easily communicate and bond together under your brand.

Referral Program

Reward your members for bringing in new members. You could set this up as a traditional affiliate program and pay out either a one-time fee for each new member or a longer term pay out for the life of the member. The point is that your existing members who love you are your best customer evangelists. It's in your favor to find ways to let them easily promote you to their friends and associates. Some of them will want to be compensated financially, yes; however, some of them won't care about making money. Some customer evangelists simply want to spread the word, so let them. However, remember to take care of them in some way or another.

33

Reusing Content

ONE OF THE best things you can do when putting together your program is to learn how to reuse your existing content. This is important! Everything, and I mean everything, you create is reusable content that you can make money for later on. Let's say, for example, you've spent the past few months interviewing experts in your niche industry. You've recorded those interviews and made them available to your members as part of your program. But wait, now you can use those interviews that are already recorded to entice new customers. Package them up on a DVD and offer it to all new members as a free bonus when they join.

One of the best ways I've seen content reused is from Jay Berkowitz of TenGoldenRules.com. Whenever Jay does a speaking gig to a room of people, he also records the audio of himself talking so that he can go back after the event and offer it up online to his readers. That's a super-smart way to create content with a dual purpose.

34

Bonuses Rule!

IF YOU'VE EVER see late-night television infomercials from the likes of Billy Mays or Andrew "Sully" Sullivan, you would have noticed that there's always a "but wait, there's more!" offer for every product. There's a reason for that and it is because bonuses work, and work well. Consumers often get triggered into buying something, anything, when they feel like the deal is too good to pass up. That's why it's important for you to *always* have some type of bonus offer included with anything you're selling.

A bonus offer can be anything. It could be a free month of service. It could be a training DVD made up of videos you've done in the past. It could be an ebook you've written. It could be access to a private forum or community. The point is that it's a bonus. It's something that the buyer wants, not something thrown in that is unrelated. Resist that urge to add a ton of unrelated bonuses. Instead, make your bonus item almost as valuable as the main item you are selling. That way the customer feels like they are getting a deal too good to pass up.

Every time you go to sell something online, make *sure* you have a bonus item of some type to sweeten the pot.

35

A Regular Guy Becomes the King of Continuity

RYAN LEE (RYANLEE.COM) is one of those super success stories who has made a multimillion-dollar business out of teaching people how to live the life of their dreams by creating their own continuity programs from their passions and skill. As all of these success stories start out, Ryan was just another regular guy no different from you when he took his passion for fitness and began to teach that information online for a monthly fee through a few different fitness web sites. His fitness programs began to grow in popularity bringing him success beyond his dreams, earning him monthly paychecks that dwarfed his former job as a gym teacher from the Bronx.

What Ryan realized from his success in creating membership programs in the fitness category—besides finding out that gym teachers in the Bronx don't make a lot of money—was that he was really good at it. From there, he left the fitness business and began focusing on teaching others, just like you and me, how to duplicate his success and live the lives they've always wanted.

Is his story one you'd like to be able to repeat? Sure it is. The good news is that it's entirely possible if you can get off your butt and try. People like Ryan took a chance, and then found out that sometimes those chances pay off—in a big way.

36

The Tools

HERE'S SOME GREAT news for you. Because you're going to start your business on the Web, there is a lot of new technology that can assist you and get you up and running without having to hire a professional consultant to help you get it done. (If you don't want to figure it out on your own, contact me. I'm available.) Here's a breakdown of some of the tools you can use to power your member program.

Membergate

I often refer to Membergate as the Bentley solution of membership program software. If you don't know what a Bentley is, it's a very, very expensive and fancy-schmancy car. It's the top of the line product in its space. That's what Membergate is, and that's why I use it. More than 1,000 web sites use it to power some of the most successful and profitable member programs on the Web today. With Membergate, you can concentrate on making your business profitable instead of trying to figure out how to make it run. Additionally, if you've ever run a member program you will know that there's a lot of work going on behind the scenes to get it right.

Membergate offers you things like a built-in shopping cart application where you can easily sell physical products or digital products on top of your member plans. This comes in handy when you want to sell something else and you don't want to have to go out and setup an entire new shopping cart for it. My other favorite feature, which is built right into Membergate, is the affiliate program feature. Without this, you'd need to go and get a third-party piece of software or join an affiliate network. However, because it's built right into the software you can instantly and easily build a powerful network of enthused affiliates who will go out there and do the selling for you. Last, but not least, when you purchase Membergate you get a professionally designed web site built right onto the platform for you. If you are interested in the software and have some questions, just contact me and I can help answer them for you.

Sites using Membergate include:

- Zappos Insights at www.zapposinsights.com
- Restaurant Owner at www.restaurantowner.com
- Membership Site Owner at www.membershipsiteowner.com
- Strength Coach at www.strengthcoach.com
- Veterinary Insider at www.veterinaryinsider.com
- Yoga Universe at www.yogauniverse.com
- Green Business Owner at www.greenbusinessowner.com
- Barefoot Executive at www.barefootexecutive.com
- MichRX Consulting Services at www.michrx.com

As you can see, you can build a member program on just about any topic. Check out all of the web sites listed above and draw some inspiration, then go make it happen! Contact me if you have any specific questions, and drop my name when you order!

37

Got a Brand in Mind Yet?

This might be a good time for you to head on over and read a copy of my free ebook called *The $7.95 Marketing Plan,* where you can learn how to build your brand for less than the price of a pizza (http://www.795MarketingPlan.com). You should already have an idea of what type of member program you want to create. Now you need to go out and get a domain name that is going to be the brand for it. The examples listed in previous chapters are excellent case studies in effective domain name branding.

Two other options for you when starting a member program are Amember and Wishlist Member. Amember is a lower cost solution that runs on your hosted domain. It can be bolted onto any web site running on the Linux platform. (Chances are your server is Hypertext Preprocessor [PHP] enabled, most are. Check with your hosting provider to make sure.) Wishlist Member allows you to bolt a member program right onto your Wordpress blogging software installation. It activates like a plug-in on your installation and allows you to create private, paid member-only sections of your web site.

38

Affiliate Marketing

How would you like to make money by telling other people about products and services that you love? You have no inventory to maintain or no employees to pay or schedules to work out, none of that stuff. You simply use a tracking code to direct people to places online where they can buy things, and when they do, you earn a percentage of that sale. That's essentially what affiliate marketing is along with a few of the reasons why it's become so popular.

An easier way to explain it is to imagine a door-to-door salesperson. Before the Web, and still today in some cases, salespeople would work on commission-only deals with the merchants whose products they sold. A good example is the *Encyclopedia Britannica* salesperson who showed up at your front door step years and years ago trying to get you to buy a set of encyclopedias. If you bought a set of the encyclopedias, the salesperson would make some money. If you didn't buy the books, the salesperson made nada, and onto the next house they went. Ding-dong!

Affiliate marketing is just like that, except in today's Internet-enabled world, it all takes place online and uses modern tracking to ensure that the affiliate gets paid. Instead of going door-to-

145

door, a Web reader clicks on a link or banner provided to them by you, the affiliate. When that click happens, the special code behind the scenes tracks the clicker over to the merchant's web site, and if they end up buying something, you, the affiliate, are paid a percentage of that sale. Awesome!

The biggest reason affiliate marketing works is trust. When you trust someone, you're more likely to take their recommendations (word of mouth). A good example of this in an everyday scenario is when your mechanic tells you that for every new customer you send him, he'll give you $50 for the referral. So when you're at your Parent-Teacher Association (PTA) meeting and your friend is talking about how their brakes went out you immediately think of your mechanic and the possibility of earning that $50. Therefore, you go out of your way to let your friend know how much you love your mechanic, the excellent work they do for you, where they're located and, of course, tell them to drop your name when they go! That's a great offline example, one that has been going on forever.

As mentioned earlier, the modern day online affiliate program works though the passing of tracking links. A person has to physically click on a link or banner, go to the web site, and buy something, while the tracking software ensures that you, the affiliate, are paid. So how do you become an affiliate and begin to promote other people's products and services? The best way to start is to join an affiliate network. Affiliate networks are matchmakers between affiliates (you), and merchants (anyone who has something to sell). Great news! Joining an affiliate network is free.

Here are a few resources to get you started as an affiliate marketer:

- Abestweb.com—The Web's largest community focused on the affiliate marketing industry.
- Shareasale.com—A leading affiliate network that is, in my opinion, the best place to start.
- CommissionJunction.com—One of the oldest and most robust affiliate networks in the industry.

- AffiliateSummit.com—The industry's largest trade show and exposition.

Now to the hard part—building an effective affiliate marketing strategy that will help you fill your pockets with juicy commissions. One of the best ways to get started right away is by using what you already have. In this case, it could be your blog.

Optimize Your Blog

The biggest bloggers in the world have realized that they can make more money promoting affiliate products as opposed to other options. Why? Because if people trust you, you can make lots of recommendations and people will act on them. Hopefully you've built up a wonderful audience of people who trust you. Now you can integrate recommendations into your everyday blogging. Recommendations that will get you paid. However, there is a right way and a wrong way to do this. The right way is to fully disclose your affiliate relationships to your audience and only promote the products and services that you actually like and/ or use and that your audience cares about. The wrong way is to fill your blog with links and recommendations to products and services that are crap, and aren't interesting to your readers. This is common sense, hopefully. The point is, don't just start writing blog posts to try to push your affiliate links. Your audience will see right through that, and before long, they'll be your audience no more. Work your affiliate links into your regular blogging habits when possible.

Another thing to watch out for is that the Federal Trade Commission (as of December 1, 2009) has put in some rules about recommendations you need to be aware of before proceeding. The bottom line is this—to make sure you're covered and not open to fines is to always disclose your affiliate relationships. The best way to do this is to include a disclosure policy on your blog. Visit Disclosurepolicy.org to use a free tool that will help you build one.

39

Social Media

Here we go, yet another pundit telling you about how awesome social media is, how it's changed the world, how everything will be different, how traditional media is dead, and blah, blah, blah. I admit it, I believe some of that stuff, and yes, I'm going to talk about some of it in the pages that follow. However, it's not going to be my primary focus. Instead, I want to talk with you about how I use social media as a business tool, and how you can do the same. Also about how you can use social media to generate attention for your business or brand and how it is going to help you spend less money on advertising.

We will also discuss how you can use social media to create attention. To do all that, the first thing we have to do is get something straight.

This Is Business . . . Not Play Time!

Perhaps one of the most important lessons to be learned about being successful online is that while the Web was at first a place for people to hang out and socialize, it's not that way anymore. Okay, it still is and can be, but if you're coming at this from the perspective of business you have to think differently. Success on the Web means that you need to use Web tools as business tools. Of course, things like social media were not designed to do business, but smart marketers and businesses now realize that they can absolutely be used as such. Too many people deride the possibility that social media can be used in this way, to their detriment.

Stop looking at things like Twitter, Facebook, and LinkedIn as time wasters, and instead as valuable—and free—tools that can help you build your brand, share your messages, and help you generate sales, leads, and publicity in a *huge* way. There's a switch that needs to be flipped in most people's heads that finally convinces them that, in fact, this social opportunity can change their success to fail ratio. So snap out of it! Once you do, you'll be on your way to meeting your goals faster and cheaper than ever before.

One of the reasons it's so hard to make the mind-set switch and begin using social media is because the old way was so much easier. In the past, if you wanted to get the attention of a lot of potential customers, you simply wrote a check to your local newspaper or radio station for some ads. Then people would read or hear your message and come running into your arms with open wallets. Alternatively, you might have dropped thousands of dollars on a TV spot because that's where the eyeballs are. Makes sense, I know, and you shouldn't stop doing it completely if it's working for you. However, know there are other ways to get it done, with social media being at the top of that list.

You know why you liked doing it the traditional way? It was easier and, therefore, you want to keep it that way and I understand that because it makes sense. In addition, it worked. You wrote the check and customers came running. However, that model is changing or, shall we say instead, moving. Social media is a much harder game, for sure, but the benefits outweigh the work involved if done correctly. The thing about social media is that you can do it yourself, yes, but it takes time and effort. Imagine being able to build your brand without having to pay a

PR firm hundreds of thousands of dollars in fees. Now you can do it yourself faster, cheaper and, heck, probably for free!

If you opt out of social media, don't be surprised when your competitor begins connecting with customers using social media and now spends a tenth of the budget that you do on marketing. Instead, the competitor spends all of that money on product development. In the end, you're toast. Did you realize that Pepsi decided to forgo spending money on a Super Bowl ad in 2010 and instead spent that $20 million on a social media campaign? That's a fact, and a clear sign that the landscape is changing.

Fact: Everyone has a lot more time than money. Your business is not always going to have that gigantic marketing budget to spend to get customers. At some point the budget is going to get cut and what you're going to be left with is your time. In a down economy what's the first thing to go out the window in most businesses? That's right, the marketing budget.

I know what you're saying, "I'm busy enough already. How am I going to spend any more time doing social media?" So let me ask you this question, "Would you rather spend $100,000 on a traditional media campaign out of your budget, or would you rather take that $100,000 and invest it back into your company and instead spend a few more hours a week working to get the word out through the Web?"

It's your choice, but you already know the answer.

40

Can I Use Social Media to Make Money?

So HOW CAN you use social media to get attention and then produce revenue? Did you notice I said, "get attention" first, then "produce revenue?" I usually get a blank stare when I ask people how they're currently using social media. Small businesses don't get it, heck, most people don't get it, and rightfully so. It's all so new. However, it does work and you can get onboard. It's still early, and the opportunities are endless. What social media brings to you is the ability to create awareness for your business or your brand. It's not something you should expect to use to drive direct revenue, although that is possible.

One of the earliest uses of social media was as a customer support tool. Probably the most famous story is the one about the Comcast cable employee who fell asleep on a customer's couch. The customer videotaped the man sleeping and uploaded it to YouTube for the world to see, generating a firestorm of viral video views with the ensuing blog posts and word of mouth. Ouch, that's a brand hit. However, Comcast made everything better by being one of the first to get onboard and use social media, Twitter in this case. Frank Eliason is easily the most famous customer service manager in the world these days because he came up with the idea of using Twitter to interact with customers.

Twitter helps companies quickly and cheaply answer questions and respond to customer complaints. Its use as a customer service tool has enhanced current customer service systems, which has eased the load on call centers, which helps ease the load on costly mistakes and disgruntled customers.

Here's how they do it. It's pretty easy to do, and you *can* do it, and you *should* do it.

- **Do it.** Get a Twitter account. What is Twitter? Just go to twitter.com, make an account and find out. Another option is to search Google for "What Is Twitter?" Create an account for your business or brand.
- **Listen.** Go to Search.Twitter.com and do a search for your business name. Congratulations, you've just tapped into a real-time conversation people are having about you. Now what?
- **React.** If you find a conversation online about your business, follow the person then engage them and offer to help them solve their problem.
- **Wash, rinse, repeat.**

Big companies with thousands of customers may choose to hire staff to do these types of things, but chances are you're not going to do that. Tweetdeck (download for free at Tweetdeck .com), or any of the Twitter third-party tools that exist today makes things easier. Tweetdeck allows you to monitor Twitter all the time. I set up custom searches for my name, my competitors' names, and any other terms that are pertinent to my business or industry. The Tweetdeck application stays up on my screen all day long allowing me to react when needed. No, you don't have to stare at it all day. In fact, you don't even have to check it constantly, but definitely pay attention to it at least once a day when you first create your account.

Since Comcast first led the way, corporate giants such as Dell, PepsiCo, JetBlue Airways, Whole Foods Market, and others, are beefing up direct communications with customers through social media tools, such as Twitter, Facebook, and YouTube. Therefore, why can't you?

You have to use social media. The days of having a wall between you and your customers are long gone. Besides, don't you want to know exactly what your customers, and potential customers, are saying about you? How much did you or your company pay for focus groups last quarter? How much do you shell out to companies to research what your customers like and dislike? There's no need to pay for that information anymore. It's all here, in the giant cloud of social media, ready for you to pluck out of the air and use to your advantage.

Unfortunately, Twitter is not going to replace your phone or e-mail. There are only about 3.5 million people on Twitter at this moment, leaving a wide gap between the majority of your customer base and those early adopters. Mind those numbers; however, they are growing at an enormous pace.

Now maybe you're thinking "this won't make my business money" and you'd be right, sorta. In the case of Comcast, the media coverage they've received has been worth millions in branding, and, of course, fewer canceled customers and the obvious cost savings from having better support. Again, revenue is not always defined specifically as sales. In the case of BlendTec and their Willitblend.com campaign mentioned later in this book, it was a direct 700 percent increase in sales. Therefore, as you can see, it can work in multiple ways. The point is that it does work.

There are other indirect ways to monetize social media, with customer service being one of those. Another way businesses do it is by lead generation. A recruiter lives and breathes on LinkedIn, building a massive base of potential referrals they can tap into. Sports betting information sites monitor Twitter for people talking about sports, then actively begin conversations with those people, with the eventual hope they will bring in new leads or customers. Restaurant owners create video blogs featuring their chefs teaching potential customers how to cook a medium-rare steak, then upload those videos to their Facebook fan pages making their fans drool all over their keyboards.

Lewis Howes uses social media to build his brand, sell his books, promote his products, and drive thousands of dollars into his bank account. Okay, so do countless other people just like Lewis, but what is really interesting about the way Lewis does it is he generates revenue online and offline. How do you use social media to generate offline revenue? What a concept! Lewis is the creator of several LinkedIn networking groups that he created for free within LinkedIn. For example, I met Lewis because I joined his Cleveland LinkedIn Networking Group back in 2008. More than 10,000 regular people like you and me, but who live in the Cleveland area, joined this group to hopefully network with one another, possibly looking for career advancement and/or to generate new customers. Once every few months, Lewis creates a live event at a local restaurant, which brings in 500 or so people. He then charges a cover fee at the door (cha-ching!) and, of course, sells his LinkedIn book (cha-ching part deux!).

As you can see from Lewis's example, you can use social media to attract customers just as well as you can use it to spread the word.

Of course, the lowest-hanging fruit when talking about using social media to generate attention is blatant self-promotion. I've always said, "Everyone's a social media purist until they have something to promote." It's true and it is called "social" media. It's the same as if you had a party at your house and you were talking to your guests in your kitchen, except you're doing it online. It's the act of people getting together and communicating, and when you communicate you often talk about your own stuff. You tell your friends about your trip to Cabo, or how much you love the new foot cream you're using. You're socializing! There is nothing wrong with that.

However, there's a flip side to that. Imagine at the same party, if you walked up to every single person and tried to sell them something. That's the last party anyone will ever come to. Remember your friend who got into Amway or Mary Kay and kept wanting to stop over and chat? You quickly found out that "chat" meant, "I want to get you in my network to buy some of my products." Social media works in the same way. You're not going to have any success constantly promoting. Resist the urge to over promote.

Of course, that's exactly what you're doing when you make a Facebook page, or when you post to Twitter that you've just uploaded a new blog post or video to YouTube. Those things are okay, in fact, those types of posts are probably the reason why your fans and followers connected with you in the first place. Understand there is a difference between talking about the things you are doing and trying to get someone to click on your affiliate link so you can make some jack.

Just like when someone signs up for your e-mail newsletter, or on Twitter, they are subscribing to your content. Tweets, e-mails, Facebook updates are all content. Don't make apologies for the things you put out there. If they don't like it, they can obviously unfollow or unfriend you at any time. Remember, this is business, not playtime.

I follow lots of businesses on Twitter because I like to get updates about what they're doing or products or services they offer. @Fatwalletdeals on Twitter offers me deals, coupons, and discounts on a variety of products. @mashable sends me updates on new stories they post. @Clevelanddotcom is the Twitter account for my local newspaper (*The Plain Dealer*), so I get instant updates on what's happening in my city. And on and on. The point is that you should create a Twitter account to do the same thing. You should create a Facebook page for the same reason. Your customers are either going to choose to get that information from you in that manner, or they're not. Remember, it's their choice. Some people *only* want me to contact them through Facebook. Some people *only* want me to contact them through Twitter. As a businessman, I consider it my responsibility to ensure that I give them options on how *they* want to communicate with me.

Look, it's a lot of hard work to use social media to make cash, but it is possible. As mentioned previously, the reasons that many don't want to try it is because they don't understand how to do it, and then when they do, they realize how frigging hard it is. Even a large business like Dell only makes a tiny amount of revenue—compared to their online retail sales that produces billions—from direct social media tactics.

Keep an eye out for new opportunities to connect with your customers as well. Every day, new social networks of all different shapes and colors come online offering us more and more options. FourSquare & Gowalla take it a step further and offer us the ability to connect with people within our local areas. For a business that makes its living off of customers within their region only, it only makes sense to be tapped into as many people as possible within that area, any way you can. For an updated list of social media web sites to monitor visit AttentiontheBook.com.

41

Need a Job, Try Facebook

LIKE MOST COLLEGE graduates, Marian Schembari needed a job, and fast. It was May 2009, right in the middle of the recession in the United States, which meant that jobs were scarce. So not only were there not a lot of jobs to be had, there were ten times as many unemployed professionals also out there competing for the same gigs. Three months went by of sending out resumes and scouring the online job portals, yet no job magically appeared for her to snatch up.

That's why Marian decided to try something different. "After three months with no results whatsoever I pulled a 'guerrilla marketing' strategy and started marketing myself and stopped applying to jobs all together," she said. "In about a month I was hired."

That's the short story. Here's the longer version of how she did it. Marian realized that she needed to find a way to stand out and get attention if she was ever going to land a job. Therefore, instead of doing what everybody else was doing, you know, sending out resumes and applying to jobs online, she decided to zig instead of zag. Marian created a Facebook advertisement. "I wanted to get into publishing so I put up Facebook ads on the profiles of employees of all the major publishing houses in New York."

> **Tip:** One of the best things about Facebook is that you can search profiles of hundreds of millions of people with the click of a button, or create an ad targeting a tiny subset-specific group of people based on their profiles. Look what Marian did. She was able to easily target and promote her ad to people inside the industry she was looking to get hired into. Why can't you do the same thing? Oh wait. You can! What's stopping you from spending a few bucks to create a Facebook ad to target one, or a few, specific people you need to get the attention of? Right, nothing is stopping you. Go do it now at Facebook.com/advertising.

Here's what the ad said:

> **I want to work for XXX** (insert Publisher here)
>   I'm Marian. I recently graduated from Davidson College. My dream is to work for HarperCollins. Can you help? Click to see my resume.

An employee of HarperCollins noticed the ad and wrote about it on the Harper blog. Here's what she wrote.

> **Will Somebody in Publishing Please Hire This Woman? And Why I Think Hyper-Targeted Internet Ads Are a Fine Price to Pay for Getting to Use Facebook for Free**
>
> The publishing industry desperately needs people with these skills: creative, innovative, risk takers who know how to work the tools of the Internet and aren't afraid to use them.

I discovered Marian Schembari yesterday when I noticed her ad on my Facebook page saying she wanted to work at HarperCollins. How clever. I clicked through on the ad and found the most awesome "2009" resume. A few hours later, I saw a screenshot of this ad on another HarperCollins employee's Facebook page with a note saying, "Uh, this is kind of scary." Of course, I had to chime in with my 2 cents.

Not scary at all, I countered. I think it's creative and innovative and blah blah blah. On and on I went, to which she replied that it's the Facebook tool of using her personal information to target ads to her that she finds scary. I must point out that we both have the fact that we work at HarperCollins as part of our Facebook profiles—so I'm not sure Facebook has used anything we declared as private for this woman to be able to target us with her campaign. I'm sure what's fair game information is all in the fine print of Facebook. The conversation went on a few more rounds with others chiming in about the brave new world and their thoughts on targeted ads, and so on.

Here's the bottom line for me: I would so much rather have an ad that is targeted to me than some spaghetti on the wall generic message that I could care less about. Please, give me an ad about a book or someone in publishing rather than make me endure a laundry soap commercial or car ad or any of the other products that I care nothing about and yet am held hostage to as the price to pay for consuming traditional media. Hyper-targeting is one of the many advantages that Internet media has over traditional media platforms, and is a modern day gift to marketers. It's Nielson ratings versus Google Analytics—and it's why I think Facebook and Twitter and all of the other free platforms that we use are going to be just fine in the new economy.

Now if marketers could just be as fabulously creative and interesting with their targeted ads, we could all be happy and prosperous.

Now that's some good attention, no? The ad, then resulting coverage of the ad, hit her targeted audience square in their foreheads, ensuring there was no possible way they could ignore her.

The result for Marian was that she did get hired by Harper-Collins on a freelance basis, and did find a full-time gig with another firm later. But what she really got out of the experiment, that was beyond value was hundreds of contacts from people who are in the industry who loved her story and initiative. So now Marian went from being just like everyone else to being "That Girl." All of this from taking a chance and trying something different and attention getting. What are you waiting for, an invitation to be different? You just got your invitation, so open it up.

42

More Power to the People (on Facebook)

COLIN DAYMUDE KNEW that if he was going to help save his local library from going under he was going to need to create quite a big pile of attention. The Board of Commissioners and the Library board had made their case and were adamant they weren't going to back down from their plans of shutting down this specific library branch. That was until Colin took matters into his own hands using Facebook and the power of the community to change things.

Colin created a Facebook page to help create awareness for the campaign. The town that Colin lived in was only populated by 4,000 people, but within a few weeks he was able to get 6,000 people behind him on Facebook, all actively promoting the save the library campaign, and helping organize it. "I'm someone who has never gotten involved in anything like this," said Daymude. "But when local politicians were obviously covering up for years of fiscal mistakes and it affected my community, I had to. I do have significant experience working with some of the world's top direct marketing experts and I used that knowledge and put it to good use. Facebook was the perfect vehicle to help me get it done."

Over a 3-month span, the community held rallies, sent e-mails and letters, made phone calls, and attracted some outstanding media coverage from local TV affiliates. In the end, Colin and his troupe of evangelists won the fight. Because of the massive outreach, pressure, and awareness put on the local government about the issue, they were able to change policy, making sure things like this couldn't happen again. There is no doubt that Facebook was the key piece that allowed Colin to organize so many people for the cause.

Some say that social media has made us less connected in some ways, but when it comes to stories like this, it's obvious that is not true.

Fact: More than 80 percent of this book research was done using social media. We aren't forced to look for our news anymore. It finds us. Social media changed everything.

Social Media Fund-raising Gets the Word Out, and the Donations Flowing

The advent of social media has also changed the way fund-raising works and how attention is given to things that might not get noticed as easily before it. Of course, that's always been one of fund-raisings biggest problems: Telling the world about your cause and making them care. That's why big organizations like the Red Cross always seem to get the bulk of charitable contributions, because they always had the most marketing to get the word out to the public. However, not anymore.

The Web has changed the way that people donate, and social media has enabled even the smallest of charities to use tools and people to drive awareness for them. It's no longer necessary to get out the checkbook and send it in the mail to your local United Way branch. You can now just go online and do it there, and because it has become easier, it has become more successful. Easy = success, remember that.

Tweetforals.com is a web site created by Quicken Loans that helped raise $10,000 in 10 hours for the fight against ALS (Amyotrophic Lateral Sclerosis, Lou Gehrig's Disease). The web site enabled people to donate to the cause, but more important to the success of it, easily allowing people to use Twitter and Facebook statuses to spread the word about their donations, thus allowing word of mouth to spread the message virally.

AffiliateMarketersGiveBack.com (AMGB) was founded in 2007 by Missy Ward, cofounder of Affiliate Summit, *FeedFront Magazine*, and GeekCast.fm. Its goal is to raise money to support breast cancer research, treatment, awareness, and community programs through combined efforts within the Affiliate Marketing industry. Since then, through various fund-raising efforts, including many walkathons, multiple silent auctions, and other goofy fund-raising stunts, such as auctioning the real estate on her "assets" to the highest bidder, Missy has helped raise more than $150,000 for organizations, such as The National Breast Cancer Foundation, Susan G. Komen for the Cure, and the Avon Walk for Breast Cancer. You were right to assume, her "assets" means her boobies, and she actually calls them boobies (that's her word to describe it, not mine). The first rule in advertising is buy space where the eyeballs are. Missy uses social media marketing to advance her fund-raising efforts, including her blogging efforts on AffiliateMarketersGiveBack.com, MissyWard.com, Twitter, and Facebook.

Cancer fighter Drew Olanoff decided to auction off his Twitter username (@drew) to raise money for the LIVESTRONG Foundation. He probably thought he'd be able to raise a few thousand dollars from his efforts, but what he didn't realize was that actor/comedian/celebrity Drew Carey (@drewfromtv) wanted in on the action. At first Carey bid $25,000 for the @drew username, but quickly pledged up to $1 million, if they could reach 1 million followers on the account. This is not a bad way to raise awareness and money. Carey says he'll "pro rate" the donation, so if he only gets to 500,000 followers, he'll donate $500,000.

A Twestival or Twitter-Festival is a global series of events, organized by volunteers around the world under short timescales via Twitter, which brings people offline for a great cause.

There's an application called Causes on Facebook that can help people from all walks of life have a positive impact on the world in which they live. The application allows Facebook users to organize into communities of action focused upon specific issues or nonprofit organizations. So does it work? Love without Boundaries is a small nonprofit made up of an all-volunteer staff. They provide medical care to orphans in China in hopes of readying them for adoption. The Causes application allowed them to beat out many better-funded nonprofits over a 50-day span by raising $144,898 from 4,115 donors.

All of these efforts work because online social networks offer a never before seen opportunity for organizing people around movements. Tools like Causes and Twestival allow us to spread the word to friends of friends and acquaintances and help us mobilize them all for a collective action. Now that's power! Imagine what your business could be doing to help support a good cause, and at the same time, build brand awareness for your firm. All with essentially the push of a few buttons.

43

Attention! Videos Can Make Money

MAKE NO DOUBT about it, online video is big business. Video, by its nature, is an easier and more entertaining way to consume content. Reading, whether it is on a piece of paper or on a computer screen, is still considered to be work by many people. We live in an ever-growing world of human beings that are glued to their computer screens and iPhones and are feeding off of massive amounts of multimedia-related content such as videos. In fact, if you take a quick look into the future you can clearly see that video content is beginning to dominate the Web from your office or den computer to your smart phone.

No, television isn't going away. In fact, according to officials at YouTube, the average user only spends 15 minutes a day on the web site. Compared to television, which the average person spends 5 hours watching, you can see that this is true. However, the times they are a-changin'. E-marketer reports that 72 percent of U.S. Internet users watch video clips monthly making video bigger than blogging or social combined. No doubt, the new frontier is going to be online video.

The question for you, as a small business owner or personal brand that seems to be lagging behind everyone else when it comes to producing your own video content, is why? Perhaps it's the fear of being on camera or the perceived exorbitant costs associated with creating video. Maybe you simply don't believe it can be effective and that it's a waste of your time. Let's dispel the myth right now. First, let's discuss the power of YouTube and show how regular people are using YouTube to make millions.

Julia Nunes was an average college student one day and a profitable recording artist known by millions the next day. How in the heck did she do that? The answer for her and millions of others like her is, of course, YouTube. While many of us scramble to create web sites, blogs, and white papers about our businesses and brands, millions of others are focusing their attention on creating video content and using YouTube and other online video sharing sites to deliver it to millions. Here's the kicker, they're doing it without marketing budgets, and they're making big bucks from it.

YouTube, which is owned by Google, is already the number two most searched search engine on the Internet (behind Google, of course). That means that today trillions of people are actively searching the Internet for video content. That also means that because of the public's fast-growing massive hunger for content in video form, regular people and businesses alike are now able to profit from the creation of that said video content.

Profit they surely do. Julia Nunes (see some of her videos at www.AttentiontheBook.com) happened to have a skill for singing, songwriting, and, of all things, playing the ukulele. Before YouTube existed, Julia was restricted to the constraints of the traditional media and the usual suspect list of gatekeepers, such as TV producers, newspaper and magazine editors, and radio show call-in screeners or disk jockeys. In other words, there was a very slim chance that anyone would know who she was and how talented she is. However, YouTube changed all that. YouTube allowed Julia to display her talent online and showcase it to the masses for free, and she did. Now millions and millions of people have watched her videos making her a genuine YouTube star.

What's even more interesting is that Julia, and many others we'll mention in this book, have been able to take that fame and exposure and turn it into revenue and publicity. Yes, actual money-in-your-wallet type revenue and publicity that would only be achievable by spending tens of thousands of dollars with a public relations firm. Who wouldn't want to get more money and more publicity without spending a dime?

Julia has been able to leverage her fame to promote her albums, which she sells online by promoting her web site in her YouTube profile. Combine that with her revenue generating live shows, her appearances on stage with famous established musicians like Ben Folds, and lest we not forget merchandising of hats, t-shirts, and anything else you can throw a logo on. Think about how this success truly demonstrates the power of online video. What would it have taken for a poor college student/musician to get the word out about their music and actually sell thousands of copies of their songs before YouTube existed? The correct answer is hundreds of thousands of dollars in promotions and years of touring to get the word out, and then maybe, just maybe, some record executive would come along and offer her a contract. That's just step one to generating revenue and with YouTube, Julia did it herself, in less than two years.

Yes, YouTube has forever changed everything, and will continue to dominate how all of us brand ourselves and earn profits and publicity on the Web, and not just for people like Julia either. Aaron Zamost, a spokesman for YouTube, was quoted in the *New York Times* as saying, "hundreds of YouTube partners are making thousands of dollars a month" and that quote was from 2008.* Imagine that. Regular people with the ability to either entertain or inform us are using the YouTube Partner Program to generate an honest-to-goodness paycheck, as if they were working a full-time job.

One such top YouTube earner is Michael Buckley, who runs a show called the Celebrity Chatter show on YouTube.

---

*http://www.nytimes.com/2008/12/11/business/media/11youtube.html

Mr. Buckley has been quoted as saying he was earning more than $100,000 from his participation in the YouTube Partner Program, from more than 100 million views, including a signed development deal with HBO. Now that's entertainment, with a paycheck. How many people do you know who would be ecstatic to earn even 10 percent of that $100,000 each year by making videos in their living room?

Below are some others who have used YouTube to become overnight stars and who are using their attention to generate revenue or publicity.

Cory Williams created a video called "The Mean Kitty Song," which at the time of this writing has more than 28 million views on YouTube. According to the same *New York Times* article, Mr. Williams, or smpfilms as he's known as on YouTube, earns as much as $17,000 to $20,000 a month via YouTube. Those profits come from direct ads through the YouTube Partner Program as well as sponsorships within his videos and product placements.

Love him or hate him, the fictional character "Fred," aka Fred Figglehorn (real name Lucas Cruikshank), is a teenager who holds the honor of creating the first YouTube channel to hit one million subscribers. In addition, the Fred channel has received more than 59 million channel views and more than 380 million video views since its launch. Cruikshank has made numerous television appearances as both himself and Fred. There are no numbers publicly available about how much "Fred" has earned via the YouTube Partner Program, however, with more than 380 million video views it has to be assumed the revenue is significant, especially for someone who is under 18-years-old.

Nataly Dawn and Jack Conte of the band Pomplamoose used the music videos they uploaded to YouTube to sell more than 20,000 songs online (in a month) without having a record deal, or even an album. The attention they received has prompted calls from major record labels like Warner, Sony, Universal, and Atlantic Records.

Mike Polk, a Cleveland comedian, created an Internet sensation with his comedy show called "Man in the Box" where he plays a disgruntled office worker constantly tormented by the characters he works with. Polk's "Hastily Made Cleveland Tourism Video" has been viewed millions of times and has landed him spots on radio talk shows and major network pregame shows. Oh yeah, he makes money on YouTube from the ads too.

The family who filmed their children excitedly opening up a Nintendo 64 on Christmas morning and uploaded it to YouTube has since been viewed millions of times, interviewed on the *Today Show*, and featured in a BMW commercial.

Actress/singer/songwriter Amy Walker is damn good at imitating accents, so she displays that skill in her videos and posts them for the world to see. Her video on YouTube "21 Accents," has gone viral with millions of views, helping drive brand awareness leads and traffic to her web site at AmyWalker Online.com. The video is 2 1/2 minutes long and features Amy doing accents from the UK, Ireland, Italy, Germany, Czech Republic, Russia, France, Australia, New Zealand, and around North America. It's great entertainment and fun to watch and definitely shareable, and that's what makes it viral.

Where in the hell is Matt? Who cares? Oh wait, millions care. If you've never seen the famous Where in the Hell is Matt video, you're missing out on an amazing story that took a 32-year-old self-proclaimed "deadbeat" from Connecticut to viral video star. The video showcases Matt traveling the world to more than 42 countries and performing his same goofy dance in each location, all backed up by an inspirational ballad. While the video never made him rich beyond his wildest dreams, he did get Stride gum to sponsor his second trip around the world with another video.

Speaking of dancing, Judson Laipply is credited with having the most viewed video on YouTube, ever. For the record, that's more than 100 million views, and counting. The Evolution of Dance shows him performing a litany of wacky and provocative dance moves to some of the greatest songs in rock and roll history. Judson has parlayed his viral success into working as a motivational speaker, author, and comedian. He's been featured on more major media shows than it is possible to mention, and continues to perform his dance before thousands of people every week through keynotes, workshops, assemblies, or trainings. **Note:** Because the music used in The Evolution of Dance video was copyrighted, Judson was ineligible to become a YouTube partner, leaving him without an opportunity to earn hundreds of thousands in revenue. Remember that the next time you think you're making a video that could go viral.

Did you ever want to ask a ninja a question? The popular YouTube channel appropriately named "Askaninja" features a man dressed up in a ninja outfit answering questions in a comedic style. Besides the profits generated from advertisements from the YouTube Partner program, this comedy and writing team have leveraged their attention for Hollywood scriptwriting contracts and merchandising.

And on, and on, and on. Every day a new story appears about someone using the attention-getting power of online video to build a brand or drive revenue, or both!

Of course, the credit really needs to be split between both the YouTube content creators and YouTube itself. Without either, there would be no successful stories to speak of. YouTube deserves the first round of credit for the creation of the YouTube Partner Program (YouTube.com/Partners), the system that allows anyone to earn a living off the ads in the YouTube Partner network. The network works like this:

- You sign up to be a YouTube partner. By doing so, you agree that you own or have rights to all of the copyrighted information in your video. That includes sounds, music, images, video clips, and so on.
- YouTube then places advertisements over your videos in a contextual format. That means that they look at the title and description of your video and try to place ads that are relevant. For example, as a YouTube partner if you uploaded a video called "The Top Ten Tricks to Doing Your Taxes," then YouTube would match your video up with an advertiser like TurboTax or TaxMama.

- Viewers see the ads during the video. If they click, the advertiser pays a cost per click (CPC) and the YouTube partner takes a small percentage, or cut, of that fee. Oh yeah, YouTube takes a small cut too. That's how they make all of their money. Exactly the same at Google Adwords/Adsense, except they're video ads on YouTube.

YouTube has said on their blog, "In the future, everyone will monetize their 15 minutes." Indeed, it appears they meant it.

What's even greater about YouTube is that they have made it even easier to promote your "outside of YouTube" content, like your blogs, web sites, and landing pages. The introduction of YouTube Annotations allows video creators to add call-to-action type bubbles or pop-outs that appear on top of your video at the points you specify. Therefore, if you were talking about your product in a video, you could add an annotation that said something such as "For more information on this product, visit www.ProductName.com" or something like "All YouTube viewers get 25 percent off this product by visiting www.ProductName.com/specials."

Of course, YouTube annotations don't let you link outside of YouTube, which greatly diminishes the effect of instant impulse clicks. However, you can link annotations to any other videos inside the YouTube network. YouTube does allow you to add a live working link in your description if you include the entire Uniform Resource Locator (URL) with the http://. A popular technique is to include the URL to your web site as the very first thing in your video description, and then use an annotation aligned just right to tell the viewer to "look over there and click."

However, what about using YouTube for your business. Sure, many comedians, musicians, and regular people have gained fame and earned big bucks from their videos, but is it possible for your business to profit from the massive exposure YouTube can bring you? YouTube has yet to focus on opening the same doors for businesses to promote their products and services. In fact, in their terms and services they specifically state that they don't want you to use YouTube to promote. That doesn't mean you can't do it, or that many smart businesses aren't doing it already, and doing it very well.

Bill Russell was at one-time a pack-a-day cigarette smoker and an overweight 40-year-old. Today he is a fitness fanatic who owns a gym called Crossfit Cleveland in Lakewood, Ohio. Crossfit is unlike other gyms in that they don't have rows of treadmills and fancy weight machines, nor do they have a cozy spa or carpeted reception area welcoming their customers. Instead, Crossfit offers a unique fitness program for the out-of-shape individual looking to get fit as well as the in-shape workout veteran who wants to continue to stay that way. No frills, just hard work, with results. Because of that difference, Bill realized it was extremely important to communicate that unique value proposition (UVP) to potential customers so they could make the decision to sign up. However, how do you do that without spending thousands of dollars on advertising or going door-to-door?

On video, that's how to do it. Bill hired a video crew to come in and tape the actual workouts and personal instruction from him and his trained partners, and then he had the video edited into a short movie that is housed on YouTube. You can find the video by searching for "Crossfit Cleveland" on YouTube. The video shows gym members lifting gigantic tires and hoisting up massive weights in various exercises. It shows real people, like you and me, sweating through their shirts, and more importantly, how much they enjoy the program and the results they get from it. It's the perfect example of how to use a video to show a potential customer what it is that you do.

Speaking from personal experience, I am now a paying member of Crossfit Cleveland and I can pinpoint my decision to join specifically to that short video I watched online. I remember first being exposed to the video by a friend on Facebook who shared the video with all of his friends. Within minutes of having watched the video, I was following Bill on Twitter, had

friended him on Facebook, was reading his blog, and had subscribed to his YouTube channel page. Oh, and, of course, I signed
up and paid him online the same day.

Attention = Revenue.

One video, that's all it took. Bill's decision to use free word-
of-mouth channels like YouTube, blogs, Facebook, and Twitter
has paid off. Hundreds of people have experienced the same sales
funnel I went through, joining up every day and sending money
into Bill's business, all without having to spend one dime on
traditional advertising. Sounds like a good plan, doesn't it.

The biggest issue with promoting your business on YouTube
is that YouTube visitors really aren't looking for "business-type"
content just yet. The majority of YouTube visitors are interested
in things like music videos, Web shows, people falling off skate-
boards, or the inevitable and widely popular Fail videos. This is
an undeniable fact and is probably one of the biggest reasons why
most businesses haven't jumped on the video bandwagon yet.

However, that doesn't mean things aren't changing and that
you shouldn't have your videos on YouTube. In fact, you *must*
have your video content on YouTube now more than ever. As
mentioned previously, YouTube is now the number two search
engine online after Google.

Following are some more important reasons why you need to
have video content on YouTube today.

Google Universal Search

In the future, all searches on Google will include a blend of results
from things like news, images, local results, blogs, shopping,
maps, books, groups, and, of course, video. This blended search
means that when anyone searches they will get a mixed result of
all of those things just mentioned. These results will be injected
randomly into the regular Google organic search results.

What does this mean for you? Well, think about this scenario.
If you sell bass fishing lures, and someone searches for "bass
fishing lures," they're going to get a blended result of products

(shopping), news about bass fishing lures, images of bass fishing lures, local places near you that sell bass fishing lures, and, of course, videos about bass fishing lures. The point is that Google realizes that the searcher could be looking for any one of those things. Search engines have grown up, and so have the people who use them. It cannot be assumed that everyone is looking for a web site about bass fishing lures; therefore, Google has to give the searcher many different options.

Without video content in place about bass fishing lures, you're losing the opportunity to expose your brand to a potential new customer.

Here's the best part, because so many businesses are not creating online videos yet, your business has the unique opportunity to get in the YouTube index and have your videos show up at the top of the list. To prove this point, take your biggest key phrase for your industry and do a search for it on Google, then go to YouTube and do the same key phrase search. What you're going to find most of the time is that the Google search is 10 to 1 or 100 to 1 more saturated than the YouTube results. That's because YouTube is playing catch up to the rest of the Web with a lack of physical product (videos) as compared to the 10 years or more of web sites and blogs indexed by Google.

This is *great* news because you have a unique opportunity to get highly ranked on the organic search results for highly searched key phrases that you probably weren't effectively able to get ranked for in the regular Google search results. This can earn you massive exposure for your brand, which ultimately will lead to more sales, leads, or publicity for your business.

Break Out of Your Box!

At some point your business is going to have to get past the "this is how we've done it for years and why try something new if it still works" stage. What videos bring to the table isn't something to write off, or haven't you been listening? Now is not the time for shortsightedness. The most successful businesses will be the ones who embrace online video right now. I once met with the Chairman of the Board of a major global health care company who told me they would never, ever, put their brand on YouTube because they were above it. As if their brand was too good for trillions of views. However, here's the kicker, after that meeting I went and looked online for videos under their brand name and found thousands of videos from their patients talking about their brand. Many of those videos were negative in nature and many were positive. The moral of the story is that your customers are talking about you in video form, and as a businessperson, it's your responsibility to ensure that your brand is represented in the places where your customers participate. If the Chairman had simply taken the thousands of existing videos they had in their outdated VCR tape collection and put them online under the company brand name, what a user would find online would be positive, helpful, brand-building, lead-generating video content, instead of a bunch of videos from disgruntled patients.

Your Competition Will Do It First

As a business owner you need to decide if you're okay with your competition beating you. Of course you're not. That line of thinking isn't appropriate at any level, across any marketing tactic or benchmark for success. So why let them beat you in the race to creating online video? If you've ever priced out search engine marketing services, you would have found out that it's not cheap. The top search engine optimization firms in the world charge anywhere from $500 to $100,000 a month for their services. How can they get off charging so much? Because search is big business. A first-page link on Google for a highly competitive key phrase can literally generate hundreds of thousands of dollars a day in sales. When your competitor's videos begin to be injected into those same organic search results, and they didn't have to pay a search firm to get it done, who's going be the winner then? Certainly not you.

44

Getting into the Online Video Game

Now that you've seen the attention and resulting benefits that Web video can bring to your bottom line, it's time to discuss how to get started making videos. Maybe you still have some issues holding you back. You should now understand how important it is for you to generate attention with Web videos, but you still have excuses . . . errr, I mean reservations about why you're not doing it.

The #1 reason most people don't want to start doing Web videos is fear. Fear of how they look on video. Fear of not knowing how to do it. Fear of the perceived costs involved. It's understandable; video is one of those things that only the experts or TV professionals do with big fancy equipment and professionally written scripts. Ah, but times have changed. It's certainly easy enough now to prove to you that video is something you should definitely not be afraid of trying out.

Fear of How You Look

It's time to get over yourself. You look how you look. Every single day people see you as you are; you! Your problem is, you don't see yourself every day except in the morning in the mirror, and watching yourself on video forces you to see yourself the way others do. Here's a tip, get yourself an inexpensive Flip camera (around $150, get one at my web site Buytheflip.com) and point it at yourself and take some video of you talking. Then watch it and do that over and over again until you're used to seeing yourself. Eventually you may want to share that video with other people. You could upload it to YouTube and keep the video private, that way you can watch yourself online and nobody else will see you, just so you can get used to seeing yourself on the Web.

Fear of Figuring It Out

To be successful at anything worth doing you're going to have to bite the bullet and figure it out. The good news is that because of the resources and technology that exists today you can get started right away without having to take a 10-week class at your local university. Back when I started doing Web video in 2006, I had the same problems as you do. I overcame them by going out there and figuring it all out. The experience I gained by trying on my own has allowed me to produce hundreds of Web videos that have brought me countless amounts of publicity and clients. The learning experience also allowed me to create my very own free online guide to help other get started called OnlineVideoToolkit .com, which has been accessed by thousands of people and has generated thousands of dollars for me in affiliate commissions and client work.

Fear of Not Winning an Oscar

Too many people still perceive making movies as something only Hollywood professionals do, but YouTube, technology of editing software, and modern equipment changed the game. YouTube has made it okay to make imperfect video; just look at the millions of videos being shared all over the Web and in their networks. Consumers are no longer expecting, or requiring, businesses to have an overproduced, professionally scored video production. Instead, as with the popularity of reality TV, consumers have accepted that "real" is in fact better.

The fear has subsided now (hopefully). You're feeling better, right? There're a few more things to consider about creating attention-getting videos you will want to know. Specifically, why certain videos get attention and some don't, and perhaps a bit about those things called *viral* videos. Additionaly, how to distribute and promote your videos once you're done with them.

Puppet Videos Got Me a Job

David Moye was a trained journalist working as an Internet marketer until he lost his job in September 2008. It was then that he decided to pursue a career in public relations, but even with some brand name agencies on his resume, he wasn't able to get noticed or get a job. Until . . .

"A friend of mine suggested I do a few YouTube instructional videos to help show my knowledge," said Moye. "I took it a step further by creating a series of skits called "PR Puppet Theatre" where I offered PR advice to my daughter's puppets in my living room."

Mr. Moye created five videos at first and uploaded them to a brand new YouTube channel called "Prpuppettheatre." Once uploaded, he began to send links of the videos out to a few media contacts. One of them was a CNBC correspondent named Jane Wells who responded by posting the video on her Funny Business blog, calling it "must-see entertainment/education for every PR flack."

The results? While the puppet videos haven't become viral by any means having only generated about 1,000 views, they have in fact gotten the attention of the right people. Smartly, Moye sent e-mails out to potential employers with a link to the videos and a note saying, "If I can get a cheesy puppet show on CNBC, think of what I can do for your clients." It worked. "One of the reasons why I was hired to my current job as media relations manager for a large PR agency with offices on both coasts was those videos, no doubt about it," he said. Since then, Mr. Moye has seen his personal brand and career stock skyrocket having been interviewed on National Public Radio and more. "It's part of my legend now. I'm the public relations puppet guy."

45

Let's Get Viral!

A CLIENT WALKS into my office and says, "I want you to make me a viral video." My answer? "I'll bet you a million bucks I can't do it." Either way, I win. If you like shooting craps in Vegas, then reaching for a viral video is for you. Indeed, there's more of a chance you're going to find a suitcase full of cash on the subway than there is of producing a video that is going to go viral. However, if you *can* find a way to produce something viral, the sky is the limit in terms of the benefits it can bring your business. All that being said, it's important to understand what a viral video can do for you.

Blenders Are Boring?

BlendTec makes high-performance blending and dispensing equipment for restaurants. Not the kind you and I use to make a smoothie in our kitchens, but rather, those expensive blenders used in fancy juice and coffee shops.

Yes, blenders are boring, or so we all thought. It's hard to imagine anything fun, creative, and attention getting to do with a blender right? Not so fast! George Wright, the man behind the WillItBlend.com campaign begs to differ. Here's the story of how

180

one attention-getting idea combined with a viral video campaign shocked the world and exploded profits.

In 2007, George Wright was walking through the demonstration room area of BlendTec when something caught his attention. He saw a big pile of wood shavings on the ground that looked out of place. Being the inquisitive type, he began to ask around to see what was happening with the shavings. What George found was the Tom Dickson, the CEO of BlendTec, would often come down to the room and jam 2×2 pieces of wood into his blenders in an attempt to break them, thereby leaving piles of wood shavings everywhere.

After investigating it some more, George realized that his fellow employees at BlendTec, who had been there longer than him, had written it off as something Tom just does. It was no big deal as most of them stated.

However, it was a big deal and as the brand new de facto marketing person in the company George knew it. If the blenders were powerful enough to blend thick pieces of wood he thought, what else could they blend? If they could blend a 2×2 and other things, what would be a better demonstration of the power and quality of the blenders than to show them blending things that, well, shouldn't be blended?

Ding! Ding! Light bulb moment!

Having only been with the company a few months, George was able to bring an outside view that most long-time employees didn't have. This allowed George to perceive the company brand differently, allowing him to come up with new strategies and ideas to present as a brand strategy.

Tip: A fresh set of eyes is sometimes required for a fresh set of ideas. Consider bringing in an outside team to take a look at your operation and see what kinds of things they can come up with. Your business is right in front of your face 24-hours-a-day, 7-days-a-week, and because of that, you probably tend to overlook the things that make your business truly exceptional to the outside world and especially to your customers.

Back at his desk, George came up with a plan that was just a little bit outrageous but was also just too good not to do.

That afternoon he walked into his CEO Tom's office and laid out the genesis for the Internet phenomenon called WillItBlend .com. "What we had was an amazing machine," said George. "But nobody knew it existed. My challenge as the new marketing guy was to showcase the brand and get the word out without a large budget." Actually, he did have a budget, $50. That's what launched WillItblend.

"I went out and bought a white lab coat, a rotisserie chicken, a McDonald's Extra Value Meal, a rake, some marbles, and a six-pack of Coca-Cola. We already had some safety glasses and gloves lying around so we just used those. Oh, and we bought the WillItBlend.com URL. That was it, that was our investment in this project financially."

Fifty bucks.

> **Tip:** You don't need to have a million-dollar budget to get creative. It's the idea that is truly valuable, and the implementation of that idea that makes it successful. What's holding you back from trying something truly outrageous and fun? Surely, it's not a few bucks.

Next George pulled Tom into the demonstration room, had him put on the white lab coat, and got him on video blending those items he had just purchased, one-by-one. When the footage came back edited they found out the real reason why viral videos work; they initiate an emotional response. In this case, laughter. "We just laughed," said George. "We had a hit and I knew it. Those first videos were posted to YouTube and embedded on the WillItBlend.com web site, and that was the beginning. It was actually pretty easy."

The Results for BlendTec and Willitblend.com

- A 700 percent increase in sales in a down economy.
- Massive brand awareness across the globe.
- Brand new revenue stream created from the advertising on the videos through YouTube and other video sharing web sites. "We started to receive massive checks every month."
- Brand new revenue stream from companies that were willing to pay to have their product blended.

However, what about the players who helped make this campaign work? Surely, they saw some return on investment for their personal brands and careers. For George Wright, the mastermind behind the campaign, he ascended (rightfully so) to a high-level Vice President position in the company. Not to mention he has been featured as a marketing expert in countless interviews for magazines, blogs, radio shows, and podcasts, which will no doubt continue to make him a highly sought-after hire for companies looking to tap into the same success he created. For the CEO Tom Dickson, he is now well known as an Internet celebrity who gets recognized in grocery stores and on planes and is asked to speak at conferences around the world.

As you can see, the benefits of getting attention and making it work extend far beyond the financial aspects. Smart people like George Wright are able to leverage their success into bigger and better things. Certainly, there's no reason why you couldn't do the same type of thing with your brand or business.

More Lessons Learned from George at BlendTec

You can listen to the entire podcast interview with George at www.AttentiontheBook.com, but here is an excerpt:

Question: What do you say to people who want to try and come up with an idea as creative as you did?

George: We were a small company with a smaller brand, so we were establishing something from scratch, which made it easier. It might not be as easy with an established brand in a bigger company. First, take a look around and find out what is awesome in your business. Really look. Then look for the new technology available to you and understand how to use it appropriately.

Question: What makes viral marketing work?

George: A viral campaign isn't the answer to marketing everywhere. It's a tool to be used if you've got the right idea for it. I'm not a viral marketing expert. I've read some books. I had never made a video to go viral before WillItblend. Our videos work because they're real, not made up. Also, because they're based on real people, specifically Tom Dickson our CEO. Finally, it has to be something people want to watch. Viral is simple. It's not complicated. Your address book is a resource to you. If I as a content provider can put something in your inbox that's so awesome you are compelled to share it, that's the definition of viral.

Question: Talk about social media a bit.

George: Social media sites are wonderful places. Viral marketing has been around forever. Now it's just online and it's easier to make happen. These sites are like virtual water coolers. YouTube is one of those places. Millions of people go to that site every day. It's a great place to put your products.

Question: Why did the videos work for BlendTec?

George: Because they're engaging. We used humor and shock. Other companies can use different things. The key component we targeted was how can we help people understand more about our equipment and the performance of it.

Question: Did anyone ever tell you can't do that?

George: There were some people who didn't like it. Some internal people and other places thought it was "okay" and some thought it was stupid. At the end of the day, the core team was comfortable and willing to take the risk. If you're working with people who aren't willing to take risks, you have to find another way to market your products.

Question: How much did you spend promoting the videos?

George: We didn't spend a penny promoting the web site/videos except e-mailing employees and asking them to share them if they liked it. The good news is they did. They loved showing off the fun video from the company they worked for. We also sent a message out to our customers, dealers, and reps.

Question: What was tipping point?

George: We posted the first five videos to YouTube, then got a micro site up, but nobody really knew it was there. A viral campaign should work naturally. Some people began to blog about it. Some customers in the blending community shared it into the passionate group. Within the first week we had millions of views on YouTube.

Tip: There are groups of communities everywhere that are passionate and that you can tap into. Do some searching in your niche, find those people, and build relationships with them. Don't just try to get them to promote your products and services. Instead, really get to know them and learn about what they do. In the end, you will find you have connected with the core voices and influencers that drive your industry, and chances are there will be a point when they will begin to refer business to you.

Question: What kind of publicity did this bring about for your brand?

George: All of sudden I started getting phone calls from the *Today Show* and *The Tonight Show with Jay Leno* asking if we could come on and blend a rake. Then the History Channel called and wanted to feature us. And many more, including the Discovery Channel, countless trade publications, blogs, radio shows, and so on. We were getting calls from all over the world. Everyone's looking for that discovery to show off to their audience.

Question: What did you think was going to happen?

George: I believed in it. I knew it was going to work. When I saw the first videos I knew it. Although I thought it might take years to get traction. But the technology proved me wrong and it took a week to get a million views on YouTube. Powerful tools are there for free. If you try them they will work for you. However, you have to change the way you think from a traditional advertiser or marketer to make it work.

Question: How much time does it take to create excellent content?

George: Financially our investment was very small. But we spent, and continue to spend, lots of time to creating content. As traditional advertisers and marketers, we've been trained for years to not create content, but to instead focus on the interruption of the content provided by TV, radio, and all other traditional media. The thing we have to realize now is that once you create content the distribution is free.

Question: What about your sales team? Did the videos help them?

George: We no longer need to educate people about our products. Now we lead with the videos. After they watch they always get it, and then it's down to the details of how to get it to them. Or they are already pre-educated by the time they get to us. They say, "I saw you on Discovery Channel or in the *Wall Street Journal*."

Question: How many press releases did you send out and how much public relations work was done?

George: We didn't spend one penny on a press release.

Question: How has the Web community embraced the videos?

George: If you search for WillItblend spoofs on YouTube you'll see a lot of user generated content (UGC) videos. We've seen people blending all kinds of things. Some of them not even using our blenders.

Still Not Convinced Video Gets Attention

Zappos, one of the largest online retailers in the world, has publicly stated they will have more than 50,000 original videos in 2010.

"Online video is another way for the customers to see the product and the company culture," said Rico Nasol, Zappos content team senior manager.

Zappos currently uses online video three different ways on its web site: (1) for product demos; (2) to open a window into the corporate culture; and (3) as instructional guides for those who want to learn from Zappos. As published on Newteevee .com.[*]

Zappos gets it. They will dominate the video search market with this initiative, driving millions of branded video views to their online web site through organic search results across Google and YouTube and in between using Google Universal Search. These videos will help them own their competitors and put them years ahead. This is also very bad news for you if you are their competitor.

The good news for those reading this book is that you don't need to make 50,000 videos, and there is still time for you to get in the game, assuming you've been convinced well enough at this point. Try this exercise now. Head over to YouTube and do a search for the biggest keyword in your industry. For example, if you're a widget manufacturer, go search for "widgets." Make a note of how many search results there are for "widgets" in YouTube. Then do the same search inside Google. Compare the results. What you're going to find out is that there are millions and millions of results in Google, and in comparison, hardly any in YouTube. This means that the competition isn't there yet. There simply aren't a lot of videos being made yet for businesses. Therefore, your opportunity is to get out there and get them made before your competition does.

---

[*]http://newteevee.com/2009/12/04/zappos-to-produce-50000-original-vids-in-2010

46

Walking the Walk

OF COURSE, I shouldn't keep spouting off about how to use video to get attention without talking about some of the ways I've done it over the years. Here are some ways I've used video to generate massive amounts of attention for my brand and my bank account.

One of the very first videos I ever made and posted online was a video of me at the dentist. The idea was to illustrate how easy it was to take video with the Flip video camera. Therefore, I brought the camera with me to my cleaning and took video of the experience. I had shots of me walking into the dentist office, as well as me in the chair with the dental assistant cleaning my teeth, all the way to me at the end smiling and showing off my clean teeth. I simply held the camera up above me in the chair and shot back down at myself. Afterward I edited the video and have since used it to feature my Flip camera mini-site (Buytheflip .com) to help sell Flip cameras. The attention I have received from this video alone has generated thousands of sales of the Flip video camera and quite a substantial amount of affiliate commissions for me. The whole thing took me about an hour.

My other mini-site, OnlineVideoToolkit.com, features 10 educational videos to help you learn how to use the Flip camera and make and edit inexpensive, yet high-quality, Web videos. The videos are accessible after registering with your e-mail address, allowing me to build a database of interested Web video makers who then get exposed to many other similar video programs and offers (all affiliate offers, of course). This method allows me to generate thousands per year in commissions, as well as build up a double opted-in targeted list of niche-specific customers who can then be marketed to over and over. Cha-ching.

What's most interesting about these videos is that they were all filmed in one take with no script. In one of the first videos, I took my video camera into Best Buy and showed the viewer what camera to buy and where to find it in the store. I then take the viewer into Home Depot and show them the exact lights I use and where in the store to buy them. The rest of the videos are shot in my office in various locations showing the viewer how I create sets, adjust lighting, wear certain clothes, how to shoot outside versus inside, and much more. Again, all shot without scripts and in one take.

In 2008, I zigged when everyone else was zagging by quitting text blogging and shooting a video everyday instead. I called the show "The Daily Flip" to help promote the Flip camera (my affiliate site, Buytheflip.com) and I produced a single unscripted video every business day on the topics of Web entrepreneurism, online marketing, success, failure, and anything else I could think of. These videos became a signature part of my brand and I became known as "the Flip camera guy." Pure Digital, the makers of the Flip camera, took notice and began to send me free cameras to give away to my readers. My daily videos were uploaded online to places like YouTube and featured in a blog post on JimKukral .com. Of course, I ended up selling a ton more Flip cameras on my affiliate site because of the cross-promotion in the videos, which produced thousands in revenue. The OnlineVideoToolkit.com web site was also featured in places like Entrepreneur.com blogs, *Inc.*, *Forbes*, Brandweek, SmallBizTrends, and thousands of other blogs and web sites.

There's simply no reason you can't get onboard the Web video game and have similar success stories. Get over your fear, get out there, and start making videos! Below are a few ideas to get you started.

Reviews

Grab a camera and your favorite product and review it! You don't need a script. Talk about the product and why you like or hate it. Show how it works and how you use it. Take that video, brand it with a link back to your web site or blog, and then upload it to YouTube. Watch as the review is viewed online and how traffic starts to filter back to your web site where they can purchase the product. Of course, use your affiliate link.

Demonstrate Your Product or Service

If you're a ball bearing manufacturer, you should take the camera back into your plant and video the process of how you create ball bearings from start to finish. Show the machines used and interview the people who operate them. Give the viewer, or the potential buyer, an inside look at what they could be putting on their shelves. Take that video and feature it on your web site or blog. Make sure your sales team has access to it and let them use it to show potential customers.

The Whiteboard Trick

You have a whiteboard in your office, right? Stand in front of the whiteboard with a pen while having someone filming you talking about your business process, products, services, or whatever it is you normally talk about in a sales meeting. Look, you do this every day for potential customers, why can't you do it in front of a camera?

Any business can do this. Web companies—use screen cast videos to show off how exactly how your product or service works.

Pool cleaners—create videos of the proper way your team cleans pools, step-by-step. Candy makers—show the customer how you create their favorite candies, all the way to how they box and sell them. Plumbers—create videos that show how you seek out and stop leaks in showers and baths. Getting the point? Show off your expertise in video form and watch as your customers begin to flock to you.

Feature Your Rock Stars

Your team is valuable. These are the people who interact with your customers day in and day out. The opportunity here is to create videos interviewing your fabulous team of rock stars and featuring them to existing and potential customers.

You Have Customer Evangelists, Use Them!

Inevitably, if you have a good product or service you have people who love to sing your praises. Those people are called customer evangelists. Send each one of them a Flip camera and ask them to take a short video of themselves talking about why they like your business so much. Let them keep the camera, heck, it only cost you $150 bucks, but just ask them to upload the videos online so you can use them as testimonials on your web site in the sales process.

47

How to Distribute Web Videos

Now that you have taken the leap to creating videos, you have to deliver them. The following is a short guide to getting your videos online.

If your videos are open to the public (not private for members or something), then you should use a free service called www .Tubemogul.com. Tubemogul allows you to upload your videos to multiple video sharing web sites all at once. You create a free account, and then set up your account to login to all the video sharing sites (such as YouTube). Then, when you have a video, you upload it once to Tubemogul and they do the rest; distributing the video to all the other web sites all at once, saving you a ton of time and energy.

The mass distribution model using Tubemogul makes sense if your goal is to ensure you get the maximum exposure and attention for your videos. However, you certainly aren't required to go this route. Many businesses choose to upload their videos to just one place, such as YouTube, Vimeo.com, or Blip.tv. Remember, you *need* to be on YouTube for the organic search inclusion but you can, and should, consider hosting your videos on other web sites or storage facilities.

If you plan to keep your videos private you have several options. *Note:* You can't put your videos on YouTube and make them private and expect to be able to play them back on your private member area. When you make a video private in YouTube that means only your YouTube friends can view it. Therefore, everyone coming to your member area would have to be your friend on YouTube and be logged into YouTube. It's not going to happen.

A better idea is to pay for a Vimeo.com plus account. For a small annual fee, you can upload your videos inside the Vimeo network and make them private, allowing you to embed them anywhere you wish for private viewing by anyone. Another option is to choose Amazon S3 storage. This simple and very inexpensive storage utility allows you to upload videos to be streamed back anywhere you wish. The biggest disadvantage is that you then need to find your own Flash video player code to embed into your web site. If you use Vimeo.com, they give you the video embed code.

If you're obsessed with the fact that you don't want to actually film and edit your own video, you could use a service like Animoto.com, which allows you build fun little animated movies with accompanying sound tracks. You can actually create something pretty decent with a little bit of effort. Pixability is another service the helps create a video for you. They send you a Flip camera and you take footage with it, then you send it back to them and they write a script and edit the video into a promotional video for you. Drop my name for a discount.

Finally, Traffic Geyser allows you to take your video marketing an entire step farther by helping you understand how to use the power of videos to generate search engine rankings and traffic, which eventually leads to more sales and leads. Read more and get links for all of the things mentioned by visiting AttentiontheBook.com.

PART

48

That Question Mark Guy

MATTHEW LESKO KNOWS how to get your attention. Chances are you have no idea who he is by name only, but if I were to tell you he's the guy on late-night TV infomercials trying to get you to buy his free "money from the government" books who wears a bright green suit with black question marks littered all over it, you'd probably say, "oh, that guy." Maybe you'd think he was the Riddler from the *Batman* television show or movies. Either way, because of how he presents himself, you're looking to see what he's all about.

Sure, he's annoying, but he knows how to get you to pay attention and, of course, how to get you to buy a lot of his books and products. Lesko has built a career and a fortune by teaching citizens how to get "free" money from the government. With books such as *Free Money to Change Your Life* and *Free Money to Pay Your Bills*, along with his outrageous persona and wardrobe, Lesko has proven himself to be a master marketer with the ability to get his customers to pay attention and open their wallets.

I once met Lesko at a trade show and asked him about his infamous suits. He said he has 15 of them in different colors (bright green, orange, lime green) that he takes around to trade shows to promote his programs and books, and in fact, he wears them out in his regular life almost every day. Being "the Question Mark Guy" is his full-time job. He's been on television for more than 20 years, and has appeared on big-time shows such as *Late Night with David Letterman* (seven times), the *Today Show, Larry King,* Joan Rivers and, of course, the biggest of them all, the *Oprah Winfrey* show, in addition to many, many more.

Matthew knows how to get your attention, that's for sure. I was able to track him down to interview him for this book. Here's what he had to say about how he did it, and how you can do it as well.

Jim: So how did you get started?

Matthew: I had an MBA in computers and I was a professor teaching computer science when I decided to start my own businesses. The first two businesses failed miserably because I was too worried about things like tax structures and logo design and all of those other things that I've since learned don't really matter. The best part is that those failures taught me how to get over it. Everyone fails. You have to fail to succeed.

Jim: What changed with the third attempt then?

Matthew: I learned my lesson. In the past I was doing what everyone told me I should do. Start a business that does this, in this way, have board meetings, and so forth. Well, board meetings suck and are boring. So I decided on two things for my new venture. Number one, I was going to worry about the customer and nothing else. Nothing mattered more than the critical success of the customer. You have a customer, or you're nowhere. And number two, I was going to have fun.

Jim: Is your success tied to your ability to stand out and get attention?

Matthew: I realized that when I had fun, I got attention. Look, being like everyone else doesn't work. Nobody's looking for "everyone else." People aren't attracted to "everyone else." When I was teaching computer science classes I had to find ways to keep those students awake. This stuff was boring! Who are the teachers you remember from school? They weren't the ones who bored you to death.

Jim: In your wildest dreams did you imagine you'd get so much publicity?

Matthew: When I first started the thought of being on the Letterman show was about as real as me walking on Mars. What I realized quickly was that it's about entertainment, not being a talking head. If I'm going on the *Today Show* to talk about government information, well, how boring is that? At home you're going to walk out of the room and go brush your teeth if that's how they pitch me in the introduction and promos. My job was, and is, to get you out of the bathroom to come and watch me, and listen to me. Even if you said, "what is that asshole talking about?" I didn't care because I got their attention. The media doesn't really care what you have to say, it's about how you say it. It's show business. They want a good show. Someone who can entertain the audience. I've been on Letterman at least seven times because they would call me to fill in for guests that would drop out. I would go sit in their green rooms sometimes waiting to get on the show. It was worth it. How much would 7 minutes of airtime cost you nowadays on major network? You can't buy TV time for cheap.

Jim: You're famous for the suits. They're bright colors and have question marks all over them. Talk about that?

Matthew: The first suit had nothing to do with my business at all. It was something in my personality that thought it would be fun to do. In the beginning I lost millions of dollars because of the suits. People thought I was being disrespectful. I'd show up for interviews and get kicked off of their sets. They thought I was a jerk. But I stuck with it. Today I *have* to wear the suit. They won't let me come on without it.

Jim: So the suits were a big part of your success.

Matthew: Not just the suits, the question marks really are more important. We live in an age of easily accessible information.

We all have tons of choices to make. Which ones stand out? You have to learn how to ask the right questions and that's why the question marks are part of my brand. Information is the easy part, but the important part is asking the right questions.

Jim: You get noticed quite a bit when you're in public?

Matthew: I have question marks on my car too. I wear something with question marks on it almost every day. People love it. I get free upgrades to first class on flights without asking. People constantly come up to me and say hello and want to take a picture with me. I will tell you though that 99.9 percent of the people who I encounter are excited when they see me. Really though, the biggest thing that makes me successful is that my products work.

Jim: What was it like the first time you wore the suit out in public?

Matthew: I was scared to death. Walking through that airport was like walking on eggshells. Putting on the suit the first time was one of the hardest things I ever had to do, but I quickly got over it after realizing the positive feedback outweighed the negative by far. The fear was that I was going to have to defend myself all the time, but that wasn't true at all.

Jim: Why does this work?

Matthew: Because I'm authentic. This is who I am. I'm not some phony pretending to be someone they're not. You have to be you or it won't work. Getting attention is about being authentic to yourself.

Jim: What do you say to businesses or brands who want to try to get attention? Any tips?

Matthew: First off, you have nothing to lose if you're starting out. You've got no business now, so what the heck are you worried about? Secondly, you have to go out and fail. The only way to succeed is by failing because nobody knows what works. Experts tell you what worked last year, not this next year. Innovate! We all have our own magic, something unique to us, so tap into those strengths and put them into play in your own way. That's what people want. They don't want copycats.

Jim: Who else does this well?

Matthew: Who impresses me? Hmm, you know what? Most businesses and people are so Goddamned boring.

Jim: How should someone start thinking about doing something that gets attention?

Matthew: Be unique and follow your heart. The only thing that will make it happen is your passion. I lost money when I did the suit the first time; lost millions of dollars, but I wanted to do it really bad. I don't mind the attention. When people come up to me for photos in a coffee shop I try to be so grateful, and I am. Thirty years ago when I had nothing I would have killed for this attention. I realize it could go away in an instant. I'm just a schmuck trying to live my life, not a celebrity. Life isn't easy. Anything you're going to do is very difficult, the only way through that is listening to your heart and doing it with passion.

Jim: Ever worry that people will only remember you as the annoying question mark guy?

Matthew: If you don't piss some people off, you're not doing anything. You're not interesting. When you're not interesting, you're like everyone else in the middle.

49

Speaking of Questions . . .

MANY QUESTIONS ARISE for businesses when they are thinking about adopting an outrageous attention-getting campaign. Obviously, one of the first questions you must consider is, "Is this a strategy that will work for my brand?" Of course, only you can answer that question, but it's immediately important to not discredit the concept, even for more established brands. If done right, it can help you accomplish your goals in a major way.

As a business owner it's often difficult to think outrageously. This is true either because it's simply not how you've done business in the past, or because your mind isn't trained to think in such a manner. However, perhaps the reason that most don't want to try something outrageous is that they are worried about how they're going to look. There is an inherent mind-set that stops most people from doing anything that could possibly make us look foolish or silly. We're taught from birth that we should blend in with everyone else and not try to be different. This is evident from the playgrounds of your youth all the way up to, and including, your personal and business interactions.

The good news is that because the majority of us are too afraid to try something outrageous, there are many more opportunities for a select few brave ones to stand out. If everyone were different, nobody would be different.

If your goal is to boost your profits and get publicity without having to pay for it, then behaving in a way that gets attention might not be such a bad plan. Maybe you're okay with continuing to spend thousands of dollars on advertising campaigns and outdated public relations tactics that rarely work. It's your call. First though, take a quick look at your budget for this and next year. What do you see? Do you have more or less money to spend on promoting your company? That's what I thought.

The big question is, "Can you accomplish outrageous marketing without turning your brand into a circus sideshow?" A valid question for sure. However, consider this before you answer, "Why should you care?"

Honestly, it's gut check time for you. Let's assume for a moment that you're in business to make money and be successful (just like everyone else). If that's the case, why wouldn't you consider any and every possible way to reach that goal? You're willing to discredit an attention-getting idea that could skyrocket your sales simply because you don't want to be viewed as silly, weird, or different. C'mon, that's your ego talking. Who cares what people think about your business or brand, as long as they're buying it, right?

Sure, you might not want to be known as the "idiot car wash guy," for example. However, consider this: what if the "idiot car wash guy," because he has created an attention-getting brand and outrageous marketing campaign, owns a successful franchise of premium and profitable car washes around the country? What happens to your car wash business when that franchise moves down the street from you, backed by a massive brand and marketing budget? That's right, you take a big hit right in your bottom line profits, because people know who the "idiot car wash guy" is. They've seen him in magazines, on talk shows, and heard him on the radio. They've heard his story and know how he runs his business, and because of that, they trust him.

They may laugh at him, or think he's annoying, but they remember him, that's for sure.

Meanwhile, he's laughing all the way to bank while you continue to struggle to run your business in the same old traditional way you've been doing for years. Does that sound like something you're willing accept, because it's eventually going to happen. Someone in your space is going to lose their ego and try something you're not willing to do. Is that going to be you or your competitor?

50

Farting Sounds Make Us Laugh, But Is Anyone Buying?

JOEL COMM DOESN'T care what people think about him. In fact, he's yet another example of a smart marketer/businessman who's laughing all the way to the bank. Joel is the creator of the iFart application for the iPhone, which has been downloaded more than half a million times at $.99 a pop. If you're wondering what iFart is, it's a fun little application created for the popular iPhone that plays farting sounds. No, I'm not kidding. Joel has made hundreds of thousands of dollars by selling fart sounds. "It's successful because it's not just fart sounds, anyone can do that, and believe me my competitors have tried," said Joel Comm. "iFart has a cool interface and a robust set of features that makes it better. That's the key to any product, farts or not."

iFart made headlines around the world during Christmas 2008 when Joel Comm made sales figures public on his blog. NBC, TechCrunch, Venture Beat, the *Today Show, CNN Money,* Mashable, the *Washington Post,* and *Wired* magazine were among the dozens of media outlets, tech sites, and blogs that featured the app, touting the fact that iFart sold nearly

40,000 copies on Christmas Day 2008. The application features a number of hilarious original fart sounds and original features, such as security fart, sneak attack, record-a-fart, and fart-a-friend. The iFart continues to lead the way of more than 200 copycat applications in the iTunes AppStore. The newest feature included in the latest update is Fart Buddies, which allows iFart owners to send fart sounds to their friend's iPhone whenever they desire. Still not kidding.

What makes Joel Comm more successful than you are? He doesn't care about his ego. "iFart is designed to be laughed at," he said. "There are always purists who don't like marketers, who secretly really wish they had come up with the idea first. The thing is, what those haters don't understand is that it goes way beyond just coming up with the idea. That's why inventors don't usually make money. It's the marketers who bring in all the cash because the marketers act on it and make it fun and attractive so that people want it."

Joel Comm's success stems from a combination of helping other people solve their problems and being in the right place at the right time, and then knowing how to capitalize on it. One of his first successes was a web site called 500Words.com, which allowed people to buy one of the 500 words on the page and then link it back to their web site, bringing you both web site traffic and hopefully some Google love. The site sold all 500 words in record time at varying prices. Price was based on the color and style of the word you created, but the base cost was $100, so even without customizing the words, which everyone did, Joel ended up earning more than $72,000 in profits in less than 72 hours. Joel then took the Web application and made it for sale to anyone else who wanted to make their own similar type of project, reaping in even more money from those that wished to capitalize on his success. Again, I'm not kidding, he made $72,000 from 500 words, in 3 days.

Joel also had a knack for helping Web publishers figure out how to display and place their Google Adsense ads on their sites to help them earn more money. In fact, he got so good at it he decided to write a book about it. *The Adsense Code*, designed and marketed to spoof the widely popular novel *The DaVinci Code*, became an overnight best-seller helping millions of people learn how to work with Google to make millions of dollars from their ads.

Why can't you be like Joel Comm? Oh, wait, you can. "No guts, no glory," Joel said. "I didn't fall into my success."

51

Mmm, Mmm, Good!

ONE OF THE best ways to get attention in an outrageous fashion is to hit the consumer right between the eyes with something they are most passionate about. Human beings all share basic needs like food, clothing, and water. Food, or hunger specifically, is something that pretty much everyone on the planet can agree on. We all need food to survive, and hunger evades no one. In the United States, we revel in the excess of food. In fact, our culture is built on excess across the board, with food right at the top of the list of things we like to have a lot of. Just look at the scores of fast food restaurants that pervade almost every street corner in our nation. There's no question: We like food and we like it cheap, fast, and a lot of it.

Restaurants make their living by bringing paying customers through the doors by any means necessary. Of course, without customers, restaurants might as well pack up their lobster bisque and go home. One of the ways restaurants generate business is by focusing on delivering specific types of food to entice the customer. We've all said something such as, "I feel like eating Mexican food tonight" at some point. Now the decision we have to make is, "Okay, where should I go?" That's when we scan our brain map for a place to go and get it.

However, what if there are five Mexican restaurants within driving distance of your location? How do you choose which one to visit? Your smart phone has determined that Mexican restaurant A has five-star reviews, but Mexican restaurant B, which is only a half mile further down the road, has daily margarita specials and homemade crab guacamole. Decisions, decisions.

It's a fierce business, especially in places like New York City where there could be four pizza joints on one single block, right next to three coffee shops, with two falafel carts 50 feet apart. How do you stand out if you're one of those places? The challenge for each restaurant is to help the customer decide to choose that restaurant over the others. Surely, they all have a plan to do that right? Well, think again. The truth is that most restaurants, and businesses in general, are run by people who don't understand marketing. It's no fault of their own. A chef is a trained to make sauces and cook vegetables, not to market what they create or themselves. Their marketing is done on the plate.

However, many successful restaurants understand that excess draws in the customer and they use it to their advantage to bring in customers and spread word of mouth. Excess could mean the size or amount of the portions or how spicy a particular dish could be. Adam Richman is the star of a popular TV show called *Man vs. Food* that makes the business of eating in excess an entertainment experience. On the show, Richman travels to restaurants—frequenting eateries that have tapped into the human psyches need for outrageous food.

Each show concludes with Richman participating in a food challenge that ends up with him either sweating profusely or preparing to vomit, or both. On one hand it's entirely gross to see anyone attempt to consume that much food or drink in such an excessive fashion. On the other hand, it's completely fascinating to watch.

What makes this show so popular, and why do restaurants offer competitions that barely anyone can accomplish?

The answer is simple, the attention draws the customer, and we all love a train wreck. All things considered, if there's a chance I might see someone try to eat a 5-pound slab of beef at the table next to me I'm more than likely going to visit that restaurant to witness the spectacle. Smart restaurants realize this, and have created outrageous eating contests that bring in customers by the thousands. Not to mention all the publicity and attention they receive from the media and word of mouth from former customers.

Here are some of the most outrageous eating challenges in America:

- Like pizza? Visit Talayna's in St. Louis, Missouri, to attempt to ingest a 30" pizza with all the fixings. Weighing in at more than 14 pounds, this challenge will award you $1,000 for your efforts, if you survive it that is.
- Hungry for steak? Make your way down to Amarillo, Texas, and stop by the Big Texan Steak Ranch for a free steak dinner, assuming you can ingest a 72-ounce slab of beef, a salad, shrimp cocktail, baked potato, and a roll in less than an hour. The challenge has been going for more than 40 years, with more than 37,000 people attempting it. Only slightly more than 6,200 have succeeded, which comes out to about one out of every six who try.
- Thirsty? The Crown Candy Kitchen in St. Louis, Missouri, will offer you a place on their wall of fame if you can slurp down five 24-ounce malts within 30 minutes. More than one hundred have tried and only sixteen have succeeded.
- Everyone loves burgers, right? Well, if you do you can grab a friend and visit Denny's Beer Barrel Pub in Clearfield, Pennsylvania, to choke down a 15-pound burger. Nobody has been able to defeat this challenge to date, yet, thousands keep coming back to try over and over again.
- It doesn't have to be the 4th of July to enjoy hot dogs! At The Corner Bar in Rockford, Michigan, your challenge is to eat 12 or 20 chili dogs in under 4 hours. If you eat 12 you can enter

their hall of fame, or eat 20 and get your meal free. However, if you can beat the record of $42\frac{1}{2}$, held by Sharon Van Duinen, you can win $500. At least a dozen people attempt this challenge per week.

- Like it spicy? At the Brick Lane Curry House in New York City, you can take on the Phaal Challenge, which is supposedly the spiciest curry in the world. Get this, the chef wears a gas mask when preparing it. People who finish the Phaal Curry get their picture on the Brick Lane Curry House's P'hall of Fame, a free beer, and a certificate with their name on it.

- Ready for dessert? At Beaches & Cream Soda Shop in Orlando, Florida, sweet tooths are challenged to eat a two-liter ice cream sundae with all the toppings, including fudge, strawberries, caramel, pineapple, almonds, Oreos, and Snickers chunks in less than an hour. The Kitchen Sink, as it's called, is usually ordered as a group, however, one person has tackled it.

- Like to gamble? The NASCAR Cafe at the Sahara Hotel and Casino in Las Vegas, Nevada, offers a 2 pound, 6 foot burrito for only $19.95. If you can finish the monstrous, cheesy entree you get it free, plus two unlimited coaster passes and a t-shirt telling the world you "Conquered the Bomb." Then you go gamble I guess?

Buuuurrrrppppp! Anyone else ready for some TUMS right about now? I know I am after writing all that.

It's important to realize that these outrageous challenges exist for one simple reason—to get customers to talk about their restaurant. Now if you don't own a restaurant, there's certainly something outrageous you can implement with your business in order to get people talking. When people talk you get attention and attention equals revenue.

Is there a grand display or challenge you can orchestrate to draw attention that doesn't make you look foolish in the process? If you're now convinced and beyond the belief that your brand could be tarnished, then you could do something like Hardee's did with their "biscuit holes" campaign. Their commercial shows people in a public setting being asked to sample two different "holes." There's the "A" holes (regular donut holes), and the "B" holes (Hardee's new biscuit holes). Of course, the video shows people candidly saying things like "The B-hole has it over the A-hole for sure" or "The A-hole tastes nasty." Crude, 14-year-old boy humor aside, this campaign accomplishes a few things: (1) It makes you either laugh or cringe; (2) It introduces you to Hardee's newest product; (3) It certainly gets your attention; and (4) It makes you want to share it with someone else (word of mouth).

Did it work? Ultimately, the consumer will decide whether the crudeness of the message will make them run to their nearest Hardee's for some delicious biscuit holes. However, there's no denying that the message was sent loud and clear.

During the 2009 Super Bowl, Denny's ran an ad offering a free Grand Slam breakfast to everyone in America. All you had to do was show up at a Denny's between 6 AM and 2 PM on certain days of the week during the promotion. In the days leading up to the promotion and after the Super Bowl the Web searches for Denny's went through the roof, and ultimately Denny's saw its traffic grow by almost 1,700 percent during the promotion.

George Naddaff was looking for ways to boost business without breaking the bank and his new budget—and without having to buy more advertising. His new food business, the UFood Grill, needed to find ways to get noticed by all the automotive traffic driving by his retail storefront every minute. He spent $2,500 on a character suit that looked like a box of french fries and then had the person in the suit standing out in front of the location all day long. It sounds really lame and not very creative, however, it made people laugh, and it got attention, and ultimately helped the UFood Grill increase sales by 8 percent. Since then more suits have been made and have been sent out to the other stores in the franchise, helping them increase sales as well.

Burger King's newest "BK Super Seven Incher" campaign sticks with the crude imagery to get attention. The advertisement ran for a limited time in the Singapore market (too racy for the United States). It featured a "mind-blowing" sandwich near the open mouth of a wide-eyed, red-lipsticked woman accompanied by the suggestive tagline: "It'll blow your mind away." Talk about a suggestive and repulsive ad. Advertising professionals lauded the campaign calling it unappetizing and misogynistic to women, and rightfully so. Nevertheless, did it work? No one knows for sure except some Burger King executive in the Singapore office. One thing for sure is that it got attention.

Here then lies one of the biggest questions we all face when deciding to use attention-getting tactics for our businesses or brands.

52

Is All Attention Good?

PUBLIC RELATIONS AND marketing pundits have been arguing this point forever. PR professionals almost always come on the "not all publicity is good" side, while pure marketing and promotions teams tend to think the opposite in that "all attention is good attention." The truth probably lies somewhere in the middle and on a case-by-case basis. There is a clear difference between the definitions of *attention* and *publicity*. Attention is an attempt to make people pay you notice to reach a goal, regardless of your message. Publicity is the coverage you obtain once the attention has taken place, and how your target market reacts to it.

You cannot have bad attention, but you can have bad publicity. They are two different things.

Case in point, it would be nearly impossible to argue that the publicity Tiger Woods has earned from his sexual escapades and infidelity has resulted in anything good for him, his sponsors, or for golf in general. Why is this the case? Because he was already at the top of his game with a well-established brand.

What if Tiger was a mid-tier, not-so-well-known golfer, who was only moderately famous? Could all the bad publicity actually

214

help his brand awareness and celebrity grow? When you're rich and famous you get publicity, but when you're not, you're getting attention, and if hardly anyone knows who you are, attention can usually help you more than it can hurt you. Usually.

We've seen people like Paris Hilton and Pamela Anderson transition from well-known American celebrities into global brands, all from the unauthorized distribution of their sex tapes. Bad attention certainly helped them.

What we know for sure is that negativity brings tons of attention. This is common sense. People love to pile on and love to hear more about the negative than the positive. If you write a blog you'll know this to be true; 90 percent of the people who read your blog will never comment. They lurk and wait for you to say something that forces them to react. Usually this involves you ranting and raving negatively about something or somebody you don't like. In fact, this is one of the best ways to get people to comment on your blog.

> **Tip:** Go negative. Be a jerk! Everyone always wants to commiserate or argue with the jerk!

However, as with anything negative, be wary of what it might get you in return. Matthew Lesko (The Question Mark Guy) can get millions of people to buy his books, but is he ever going to be invited to a White House dinner expecting to wear his bright-green question mark suit? Of course he isn't. Paris Hilton may be a global brand, but is she ever going to be able to run for the Senate or lead the United Nations? Heck no.

There's a price for getting attention in such a manner, and we should all be fully aware of that before seeking it. Going *blue*, as comedians call it, is a risk that some might not find worth taking. What you have to ask yourself, "Is your brand ready to take the heat that will most likely come from taking that position?" If you're a nice person and not used to controversy, and you're trying to *shock* people in a way that's out of character, then the blow back is going to hit you in your gut hard, and you may not recover. It's risky for sure.

Again, be who you are. If you've always been a rabble-rouser, stick with it.

53

Image Counts

THE PERCEPTION YOUR potential customer has of you is a critical part of why they choose you. It's common sense. You're not going to let your dentist put his hands in your mouth if his fingers are covered in warts, are you? No, you are not, because image counts. You're not going to buy a hot dog on the street from a cart that is broken down, covered in mud, and smells bad, are you? No you're not, because image counts.

On the Web, sometimes it counts even more, and a good photo of yourself can sometimes mean the difference between you getting the gig or not.

I sell Web consulting to small business owners. You know, lawyers, plumbers, restaurant owners, financial planners, and so on. If you have the same target customer group, here's a little tip that I learned years and years ago.

Small business owners don't give thousands and thousands of dollars to consultants who wear flip-flops, torn shorts, and t-shirts. They just don't. They want to spend their money with people who look a certain way. That's why you'll always see me dressed professionally on any of my web sites or projects that cater to that audience, because image counts. Following are some tips for creating a better image of yourself:

- Get a professional headshot. No, you can't have your spouse take it with your digital camera. Look for a photographer in your community who has a studio you can visit. This will ensure that the lighting is perfect and the quality of the photo is professional. Get the shot taken on a white background so you can integrate it into your Web designs. Make sure the photographer will provide you with high-resolution photos on a DVD, CD, or memory stick, because you may need to provide these photos to a print publication in the future where they require high-resolution files.
- Pick your clothing for your audience. If you're selling beach gear to vacation goers, then sure, it's appropriate to wear your swimsuit and flip-flops. However, if your target audience is professionals then you should dress in a business manner. You may want to bring a few different sets of clothing and take multiple shots.
- Get a haircut first! You want to look your best, as this is the image that is going to represent you for a long time.
- Use your new photo on your web site, your blog, and on your social media sites—such as Twitter, Facebook, and LinkedIn—for consistency purposes.

Icons can also be used to get attention and get you noticed. Dave Taylor of AskDaveTaylor.com used a caricature of himself on his web site as part of his brand. There's a great web site called Iconizeme.com that offers inexpensive handcrafted digital caricatures you can use across all of the places your face is shown. That includes your Twitter and Facebook profiles, as well as on your blog or web site. The advantage to using a caricature is that not everyone has one, and in a sea of regular photos a caricature can make you more memorable.

I've been using caricatures on my web sites and profiles for almost 10 years now off and on. On more than one occasion I have been told that the uniqueness of the picture has drawn the person to become part of my social circle or helped generate interest in my brand as a whole. Isn't that the goal here? The answer is yes. We all have to find ways to get noticed, and having a caricature is a good way, albeit a small way, to get someone to look in your direction. In addition, they look cool and are fun.

Your logo is also an essential part of your brand image. You do have one, right? It's not like the old days when you had to hire a brand consultant to go out and handcraft a logo for you. Sure, you can still do that, but who has that kind of money nowadays? An excellent option for you are web sites like 99designs.com and Crowdspring.com. These web sites offer you the chance to submit a design contest for whatever you need. Maybe you're looking to get a simple logo designed, or have a web page designed. Use a web site like 99designs.com to have thousands of designers create artwork for you while competing against one another. All you do is monitor the entries, pick a winner, and then pay the award.

Take your image a step further and spend some time and effort building web site and blog designs that will help you, not hurt you. If your web site looks like it's straight out of 1999, you're probably not going to have an easy time convincing people to buy from you over the updated competitor. I know, I know, you don't know how to design and build a web site. Well, web sites like Yola.com and Squarespace.com offer you a free and easy way to build a decent looking web site without having to be a graphic designer or HyperText Markup Language (HTML) coder.

54

Do You Have a Voice?

IT'S NOT ONLY important to have the right image on the Web, you also need to have a voice. It doesn't matter what you do or what you're representing, your audience needs to be able to connect with you if you want them to be able to latch on and remember you. To do that, you need to have a unique and interesting point of view or a voice. Without it, it's going to be much harder to break through and get noticed.

Joel Libava, aka The Franchise King, has a voice. He's the world's preeminent expert on the business of franchises. When he does speaking gigs and television interviews, he has his crown right next to him, or on his head. So not only is he the expert in his niche, he also has a *hook* that makes people pay attention to him. He's the king! Anyone can go on *Fox News* in a suit and talk about franchising, but only Joel can go on and engage his audience with his crown.

Let's get beyond the hook, because having a voice is bigger than that. As previously mentioned in countless examples throughout this book we've talked about ways to stand out and get people to pay attention to you. However, that's not all that is required. Your voice matters. Your voice is how you consistently communicate your messages to your audience.

Remember, boring isn't going to work. How many boring people are remembered, or even listened to? Professional public speakers make a living off not being boring. They know that effective communication is about engaging your audience on multiple levels and truly getting them to listen to you. That's when you know your voice is good; when you can look someone in the eye and see they are truly listening to you and buying what you say. That's what you have to be, practiced and perfected. There is no greater feeling to me than being in a room of people whose eyes are all glued to me, eating up every single word I have to say. I can see them nodding their heads in agreement every time I bring up a new point. That's when I know my voice is getting through.

Some would call your voice your brand, and they're right to an extent, it's part of your brand. Once you've perfected your messages and tested them out, you will begin to get noticed and remembered for them and it will then become part of your brand. Think about all the great speakers you've seen, you'll always remember them for not only the excellent information and ideas they presented to you, but also for how they did it.

Now think about some of the most talked about people in your industry; the rock stars. Most of the time, those people are the ones that know how to engage their audiences and ask the right questions. There's a reason there's always that small group of rock stars that exist in any industry, even yours. It's because they've learned how to communicate in ways that you haven't explored yet. They're doing something better, different, or more unique than you are.

Are you a fire starter? Are you controversial? Are you able to create conversations that people care about hearing? Your voice will do all of those things for you, with many benefits to boot, if you can discover it and use it. Quit sitting back and pretending that you're going to become rich and famous by doing the same thing everyone else is doing. Establish a unique voice that makes you the center of attention and discussion. There's never been a greater time in the history of the world to build a strong brand with a strong voice and get it out there and noticed. What are you waiting for, an invitation? You just got it.

When you do interviews with potential clients, the media, any gatekeeper or decision makers how you look, what you're wearing, what you say, and how you present yourself is exactly how people will remember you.

Gayl Murphy is a media expert, veteran Hollywood correspondent, speaker, media and presentational business coach, and the author of *Interview Tactics! How to Survive the Media without Getting Clobbered!* As a Hollywood correspondent, Murphy specializes in interviewing the industry's biggest stars. Based in Hollywood, she has worked with many of the top news outlets, including ABC News, BBC News, E!, and SKY News, to name a few. She's been up-close and personal with about 14,000 of the most famous celebrities and newsmakers in the world. You name them and she's probably interviewed them. In fact, she stated on her web site at InterviewTactics.com, "I can probably count on one hand the number of stars I HAVEN'T talked to."

Gayl knows a thing or two about having a voice. Here are some of her tips to consider before stepping up the microphone, or sitting down with an interviewer:

- How do I want the world to know me?
- How do I want them to see me?
- What do I want people to remember about me?
- Do I want them to think of me as funny, serious, focused?
  - If the answer to the last question is yes on all three, then make sure you bring those parts of yourself with you and share them.
- An interview isn't a confession, so there's no need to reveal your deepest and darkest secrets to a complete stranger.
- An interview isn't a conversation either, but it is *give and take*, so listen carefully to what's being asked.

You get the idea. You can't just sit down and start talking. Well, you can, but is that going to help you get noticed? Gayl's advice is paramount. How do you want your audience to remember you? It doesn't matter if it's funny, serious, focused, or anything else. The point is that you want them to know you, to see you, to remember you. Otherwise, you're just another interview. What's the point in that?

HirePasha.com

Pasha Stocking didn't let technology hold her back from getting what she wanted. The 37-year-old Connecticut woman, and a single mother of three, was laid off from her job and in desperate need of a new one. The problem was that she wasn't getting anywhere in her job search. Either no jobs existed or her current efforts just weren't paying off. It wasn't from a lack of trying either. She sent out tons of resumes, went to countless job fairs, and even applied at temporary agencies hoping to land something, anything in the marketing and design field. Nothing worked.

That's when the idea hit her. If she was going to truly break through and get noticed, she was going to have to do something unique or different or both! Therefore, she took a risk and rented a billboard on Interstate 95, a heavily trafficked area in her region. She used the money she had been saving for a down payment on a home to purchase the billboard. The billboard included a giant picture of herself with the words "Hire Me! Unemployed and Seeking Employment. Hirepasha.com." Of course, the web site directed travelers back to a copy of her story and her resume.

Did it work, well sort of. Okay, it worked, but not exactly as you figured it would. Pasha did get some responses from a few potential employers, but none of them were the right fit. What did happen, however, is that Pasha's idea set off a firestorm of publicity for her, getting her featured in *USA Today*, the *New York Times*, NBC Online, the *Chicago Tribune*, and many others.

She suddenly also became a wanted guest on television and radio talk shows. The simple act of taking a chance and getting attention created something new for Pasha, and that was celebrity. Everyone wanted to hear her story, regardless of the outcome for her and a new job, which never came.

Pasha estimates that the publicity she received from the billboard has approached $20,000 to $30,000 in publicity and public relations costs she would have had to pay out of her own pocket. That publicity and attention helped her create her own PR firm.

55

Crazy = Success Question

IT'S INTERESTING. WHEN you speak to successful people who have done something outrageous you often are told the same story. It always starts out with something such as this:

"Everyone told me I was crazy to do this."

What can you do that's crazy that just might work? Think about it.

Stupid Ways to Get Attention (Don't Try This at Home)

James Frey is the author of a 2003 memoir of addiction entitled *A Million Little Pieces*. He went on *Oprah* to promote his book after the queen of daytime talk named it to her Book Club, making it a best seller. Hold on a minute! There's a big problem here. Most of what he wrote he made up. Career over. You don't mess with Oprah.

Obviously, making things up and pretending they really happened is a bad way to go about getting attention for yourself. As children, we're taught not to cry wolf in fear that we will lose credibility, and get a spanking. We don't run into crowded spaces and yell *Fire!* for the same reason—not to mention we just know better. Okay, some of us do at least. The point is that getting attention isn't usually a good thing to get if you're getting it the wrong way.

In 2009, the story of the "Balloon Boy" captivated millions of people around the world. The story was that a young boy had jumped into his father's balloon and was carried away into the clouds, floating hundreds of feet above the ground, and in serious danger. Hundreds of volunteers raced to ensure the boy's safety and news crews from around the world spent precious airtime covering what ended up being a bogus story. As it turns out, the boy's parents concocted the entire thing in an attempt to draw attention for themselves. Maybe they thought they'd get a reality TV show from it, a book deal, or something like that. What ended up happening was that they served jail time and paid a hefty fine instead. That's bad attention, and it cost them in the end. In fact, the judge ruling on the case stated specifically that they were not allowed to make any money whatsoever from the ordeal, through any means.

Tareq and Michaele Salahi are now best known for allegedly crashing President Obama's first White House state dinner. They showed up at the event uninvited and proceeded to take pictures of themselves with Vice President Joe Biden and Chief of Staff Rahm Emanuel to name a few. Then they took the photos, uploaded them to their Facebook page, and flaunted the fact that they weren't invited guests. The media picked up on the story and brought down a world of bad attention on them that has since, at the time of this writing, implicated them in a world of criminal trouble. Speculation was that the two Washington socialites were in talks regarding a reality show (which they did eventually get). In true style, the couple is now being paid to make appearances. Imagine doing something criminal and being paid because of what you did.

We now live in a world where it's easier than ever to craft a story about our businesses or ourselves and then attract media attention. A world where if you can do something outrageous, or even stupid, you can be on CNN in a matter of hours, or less, because of 24-hour news cycles and our insatiable consumption for news and entertainment. Whether that's a good or a bad thing is not important. What is important is that it's a fact.

Combine that with the fact that humans are more than ever enticed to be famous or "be somebody" and you have a recipe for disaster. Cultivating a culture of people who seem to be only interested in being the next big thing, because if everyone knows who we are, then we can leverage that into some type of revenue. The sad part is that it's true. Levi Johnston was just a regular kid from Alaska, who just so happened to knock up the daughter of once Vice Presidential hopeful Sarah Palin. For some reason beyond logic, Levi is now experiencing a fine career as a model and actor, earning a lot of money off his fame.

Two idiots working at a Domino's Pizza franchise, in North Carolina, thought it might be a good idea to take some videos of themselves doing gross things to the food they were in charge of cooking. They stuffed cheese up their nostrils, passed gas on the pepperoni, and blew their noses on meals they were preparing. All while having a great big laugh about it on the video, which they then uploaded to YouTube. Not very smart of them, and while a few of their friends probably laughed, the rest of the world, the legal authorities, and Domino's was not laughing. Perhaps they thought they were going to be YouTube stars. The good news is that they both face criminal charges for food tampering.

National Basketball Association (NBA) super-star Gilbert Arenas thought it would be a good idea to bring a gun into a professional NBA locker room, and then proceed to pull it on another teammate in an argument about a gambling debt. All that attention got him was a large fine and an indefinite suspension from the league. Oh yeah, and a felony.

Sometimes this kind of thing works. Maybe Joe Wilson will have better luck. During President Obama's major health care speech in 2009, South Carolina Representative Wilson (R)

yelled out "You lie!" when the President said the legislation
would not mandate coverage for undocumented immigrants.
Gasp! You can't yell at the President and get away with it, right?
Certainly, your career is over, right? Well, not so fast. Two things
happened to Mr. Wilson after the fact. The first was that he
raised more than a million dollars in campaign funding from the
people who agreed with him, $750,000 of it in the first 48 hours.
The second thing was that his opponent raised twice as much.
Time will tell if his attention-getting outburst will help him get
reelected, but there's certainly no doubt that he is now someone
everyone knows about. This is another example of good attention versus bad publicity. If he were someone more well-known,
this probably would have backfired.

Dating and social network web site BeautifulPeople.com axed
about 5,000 of their members following complaints that they had
gained weight. "As a business, we mourn the loss of any member,
but the fact remains that our members demand the high standard
of beauty be upheld," said web site founder Robert Hintze.
"Letting fatties roam the site is a direct threat to our business
model and the very concept for which BeautifulPeople.com was
founded." "Letting fatties roam the site?" That kind of comment
will make news, and it did. The question that remains is if that
attention will turn into more revenue.

Ashley Madison has a dating web site that caters to people
wanting to have an affair. Yes, you read that right. They are
promoting infidelity. Just read their slogan, which is, "Life is
short. Have an affair." More than 3.2 million members suggested
that the web site is onto something, and it's straightforward,
direct approach to marketing seems to be working, obviously.
Why does it work? Probably because they're honest about their
business. Unlike other dating web sites, Ashley Madison's web
site doesn't pretend to be something it's not, and its advertisements certainly don't pull any punches either. A recent television spot shows a couple having a passionate and steamy moment
together when the title words come up saying "This couple is
married . . . but not to each other." Shocking! In another ad, a

man retreats to the sofa to escape his obese, snoring wife while a voice-over declares, "Most of us can recover from a one-night stand with the wrong woman, but not when it's every night for the rest of our lives."

Feeding Off Someone's Fame

Anyone can take an ordinary everyday product and put a famous person's likeness on it, make a quick buck, and get some attention. If you're selling condoms and trying to compete with 100 other major brands in a crowded marketplace, what do you do to stand out and get noticed? Well, one way is to leverage someone else's fame or celebrity. At ObamaCondoms.com you can buy condoms with President Obama's face on the package, which will allow you take part in the "the ultimate stimulus package." From the web site, "These are uncertain times. The economy's a ball-buster and the surge went flaccid . . . but now there's Obama Condoms, for a change you can believe in!" Endorsed by the White House? Probably not, eh? Nevertheless, a real product making its way off the back of someone famous. Also on the market in Obama-land are illegal drugs like Obama ecstasy and acid, not to mention the Obama Chia pet or Obama Chicken Fingers. Again, most likely not White House approved.

56

Why Do Some People Get Attention Yet Can't Monetize It?

IT TAKES A special skill to be able to figure out ways to reap the rewards from your attention-getting ideas. It's important to have a plan in place so that you aren't caught up in a situation where the momentum passes you by.

Step 1: Research It!

Once you have an idea in your head you first need to figure out if it's been done before. A quick look on Google can usually help you track down what you need to know. Don't just stop there though. Do searches on YouTube, as well, and other non-Google search engines like Bing, MSN, and Yahoo! just to be thorough. If your idea is something that could be considered trademarkable, then you'll want to do a quick search at the U.S. government trademark web site at Trademark Electronic Search System (TESS) (http://tess2.uspto.gov). Just because it doesn't show up in the online search doesn't mean the idea is not protected. Consult an attorney and have them conduct a proper search, which will usually run you around $500 to $3,000. There's no sense in spending a lot of time and effort and, most importantly, money, pursuing an idea that is someday going to get you in legal trouble. An attorney should also be used when you're unsure about conducting online contests or using someone else's name on your product or service.

Of course, just because it's been done already doesn't mean you can't do it better. Competition is a great motivator, and a great starting point for imitation. Chances are that the idea wasn't done as good as it could have been done, leaving the door open for you to take the reins and do it even better. Learn from you competitor's mistakes and figure out what they're doing, or rather what they're not doing, that you can improve upon with your idea.

Step 2: Act on It!

Wayne Gretsky, probably the world's most famous, and legendary, hockey player once said, "You miss 100 percent of the shots you don't take." He's right. A great idea is nothing if you don't take action on it. Ask most entrepreneurs how they got started and you'll often get the same answer, "I just went and did it" or "It was do or die." Unfortunately, not everyone is born an entrepreneur and you are as open to risk as they are.

Here's an update for you reading this right now. If you don't try, you lose. Plain and simple, you will lose. If you have an idea that you think can work, then you *have* to give it a go. Act on it and see what happens. The downside is if you never try and you never succeed. How depressing is that? . . . very.

Step 3: Be Interesting

Actually, you could put this before Step 1 if you wanted to. Justin Kownacki offers up a fabulous tidbit on his blog about this topic that sums it up quite nicely:*

---

*http://www.justinkownacki.com/2010/01/05/stop-trying-to-monetize-what-isnt-interesting

It's a sad truth that's become a running joke: these days, you can't attend a seminar, a Webinar, a meet-up, or a Tweetup without someone asking the all-important question: "How do I monetize?" The answer to that question usually involves a mix of SEO, "personal branding" and "finding your niche." These answers are intended to propagate the notion that *anyone* can make a living online, because *everyone* wants to believe that. What they're not telling you is something they haven't quite admitted to themselves: **You have to be interesting (and most people aren't).**

From the moment we realized we *could* create media and share it online, it (il)logically followed that anyone who *can* produce media (which is all of us) deserves to make a living from it. You might see the flaws in that theory, but you'd be in the minority.

Reality TV (and YouTube) has so eroded our perception of fame, success, art, and even reality itself—to say nothing of lowering the expectations (and the standards) of "what it takes" to produce media that people will choose to consume—that anyone who's ever read a book or seen a moving picture now believes not only that "I could do that," but that "I could do it better" (aka, "If the right guy at CBS would just watch my web TV pilot, I'd be banging Margaret Cho *tomorrow*!").

This delusion has driven millions of amateurs to envision themselves as auteurs waiting to be discovered. In their minds, the only thing stopping them from acquiring fame, fortune, and household-name status is . . . fame and fortune. What they don't seem to understand is that fame and fortune require money—our money—and we don't give that up unless we first surrender our attention. And there's a lot competing for our attention right now.

Precisely.

Did You Ever Eat a Chocolate Covered Grasshopper?

Grasshopper.com provides a virtual phone solution for entrepreneurs who want to sound professional and stay connected. As with most new businesses, the hardest part is getting noticed. Grasshopper knew that in order to stand out and get some buzz going, and new customers, that they had to do something different.

Their solution was to package up 5,000 packs of real chocolate covered grasshoppers and send them out to 5,000 influencers on the Web. People such as bloggers, technology pundits and, in general, people who could, and would, talk about them. The results were astounding. The campaign created a massive surge in social media mentions, Web traffic, and new customers.

Specifically:

- 4,911 percent traffic increase from April to May.
- 144,843 video views with 162 comments.
- 1,500 tweets.
- 120 blog posts in 1 month.
- 7 national TV mentions.

It worked! Grasshopper successfully saturated the blogosphere and twitterosphere, and at the same time reeling in a massive amount of mainstream media coverage. Not bad for a creative idea and some dead grasshoppers.

57

The Web Is Full of Copycats

THE INFAMOUS SNUGGIE (a blanket with sleeves) was actually created by Gary Clegg in 1998 when he was a freshman in college, except he called it The Slanket. He actually promoted the product a long time ago on places such as QVC; however, his marketing was off the mark. No, wait. He got his butt kicked by the Snuggie marketing team years later. There's no other way to put it. A good old-fashioned butt kicking.

The Slanket and the Snuggie are pretty much the same product. However, there are differences in the product and the marketing. The Slanket is more like a big blanket, while the Snuggie is more like something you wear as clothing. The makers of the Snuggie realized that you don't carry a blanket with you around the house while making toast and letting the dog out to pee. So instead, they designed the Snuggie as something you could wear that lets you stay active, even showing people in the ads wearing it outside of the house!

However, therein lies the real difference of the two products—the marketing behind them. The Slanket was marketed as a luxury item for fancy and rich people to use while lounging in their million-dollar mansions, while the Snuggie was marketed to the masses, the regular people who might be picking their kids up from a lacrosse game or driving through McDonalds for lunch. In addition, let's be honest, the marketing for the Snuggie is very kitsch, which helps it tremendously. Kitsch is a German word denoting art that is considered an inferior, tasteless copy, or worthless imitation of something extraordinary. Okay, that's the fancy wikipedia definition. Here's a better way to describe kitsch. Tacky, trashy, or even gaudy. Worldofkitsch.com, a web site featuring all things kitsch, defines it best as:

> Kitsch or kitch is originally from the German word meaning *trash* although more recently has been used as a word to describe objects of poor taste and usually poor quality.

You know, like making a replica of the painting Mona Lisa, except using Burger King wrappers and beer cans instead of paint. Maybe you've seen those painting with the wonderful dogs playing poker with a black velvet background, that's kitsch. The swag lamps that used to hang in Mr. Furley's apartment on *Three's Company*, kitsch. The Snuggie certainly falls into that category as well. It's more like something you laugh at and buy as a joke, instead of something you really, really need.

Therein lies the brilliance of the marketing of the Snuggie. It's silly, or kitsch, enough that you can make fun of it (oh, and we all do, search "Snuggie parody" on YouTube for a laugh), yet it's useful enough that you can actually sort of use it, which makes it get attention. Remember the two reasons people come online: to have a problem solved or to be entertained. The Snuggie does both, and when you can do both, you can get attention, and make a lot of money.

Gary Dahl was a frigging genius, to marketers at least. Gary is the guy who invented the Pet Rock back in the 70s. For those of you too young to remember, the fad started when Gary was talking with his friends about how he doesn't like to have pets because of the everyday inconveniences such as feeding them, cleaning up after them, and so on. He came up with the Pet Rock for those people. A pet that never needed to be fed, groomed, walked, bathed, and, most importantly, never died. In other words, the perfect pet! The 6-month fad made Gary an overnight millionaire. Dumb for sure, but let's face it, sometimes dumb gets attention.

The Big Mouth Billy Bass is a fake fish mounted on a plaque that sings songs to you, such as *Don't Worry, Be Happy* from Bobby McFerrin or *Take Me To The River* by Al Green. It's designed to work on a motion sensor so when you walk past it it begins to sing. So not only is it dumb, it's annoying to boot! Which probably explains why so many people tell other people about it and why it's become somewhat of a pop cultural icon. The toy has appeared on the television show *The Sopranos*, as well as been part of the hit Disney movie *WALL-E*.

Crocs, those big ugly plastic-looking shoes that appear to be made out of foam, were created by George B. Boedecker, Jr., and originally developed to be sold to spas for customers to wear in-between facials and hot rock body massages. Yet somehow, someway, the shoe became popular and spread like wildfire onto the feet of consumers around the globe, causing shoe snobs everywhere to yell out *fashion disaster* at the top of their lungs. First lady Michelle Obama has even been *caught* wearing a pair of Crocs. A Facebook group even exists where more than 1.4 million members have decided to join forces to find a way to eliminate the shoes. However, just because a select few think they're dumb and hideous, that doesn't mean that everyone else does as well. In 2008, NPD Market Research Group ranked Crocs as the number one casual brand in the athletic specialty sporting goods channel for women and children.

58

Customer Evangelists Rule

IF YOU'RE LIKE me you're a super fan of a select few things, which makes us both customer evangelists. Being a customer evangelist, or as some call them, super fans, means that you go out of your way to tell other people about the things you love so much. It's a business's wet dream to have a rabid fan base of proactive promoters out there spreading the word about them, or at least it should be.

Assuming you want to be an evangelist for something you love, be wary before you set out on your journey to tell the world. It can be tricky navigating between shortsighted corporate executives who have no vision or tolerance for exuberant customer evangelists and your vision for how you'd like to promote their product. I've personally dealt with this situation, having become a vigilant fan of a major hosting company. I went as far as to spend an enormous amount of time, effort, and money working on a video commercial to promote the company, only to get contacted by the company's legal representation telling me *you can't do that*, in so many boring legal words. Ugh, I guess I should have asked them if I could say how awesome they were before I did it, right?

Smart businesses embrace their customer evangelists and help them by first acknowledging them and then by providing them tools to help them spread the word. I'm an evangelist for a dietary supplement called JoeBees. It's bee-pollen that comes in capsules that give me tons of energy (I don't drink caffeine), better digestion, and helps me sleep like a zombie on NyQuil. I love this product, I will take every opportunity to tell the rest of the world about it whenever I can, and I do. Joe B., the owner of JoeBees.com, gets this and has personally reached out to help me in my quest to promote his product. He often sends me free samples to give away and has personally phoned me multiple times to just say thanks. He even booked me on a local radio station once to do a promo for his product, which I gladly did, exposing my name and brand to hundreds of thousands of my customers.

What a concept! Let me ask you this, "When was the last time you picked up the phone and called your best customers or fans?" If you don't know who those people are it's time to find out, and find out fast. If done right, before you know it you can have your own group of customer evangelists out there preaching to the world about you. Alternatively, maybe you'd just like to continue spending more and more money on advertising.

Being an evangelist means you want to tell people about what you love. It makes you feel good to do so.

That's probably what most marketers don't realize about the power of word of mouth and customer evangelism. It's not about getting something in return, it's about sharing. It's about making ourselves feel good by helping others, and a little bit about our ego. The challenge for you is to tap into that feeling from your biggest fans and help perpetuate it.

The Industry of Snuggie

Not to continue harping on the Snuggie, but because of the fun-icity (yes, I made that word up) of the product, an independent pop cultural phenomena called the Snuggie pub crawl has appeared on the scene. A Snuggie pub crawl is when a group of people go bar-hopping all wearing Snuggies. Imagine hundreds of people stumbling from bar to bar down the street in some type of drunken blanket-wearing zombie crawl, with sleeves. Now there's a picture that gets attention! In fact, it does get attention in a big way, having been featured by the media around the globe, all without spending a dime on advertising.

You can even create your own event at SnuggiePubCrawls. com if you want to get in on the action. You can join a social network that's all about Snuggies and people who love them at Snuggiebook.com, the "The Social Network with Sleeves." The rock band Weezer even had their own Snuggie for sale at Weezersnuggie.com. You can get custom Snuggies made at Customsnuggies.com. You can even get a Snuggie with your college alma mater on it at Collegesnuggies.com.

But wait, there's more! Snuggie fan sites have appeared all over the Web, all independent of the makers of the Snuggie who in no way seems to care, and rightfully so—the attention is worth a gold mine. Many of the fan sites you see online are in fact created by fans and marketers alike, and most of the time by both. Smart marketers hop onto trends and leverage the popularity of them into online communities, blogs, and fan sites for the sole purpose of making money either by sponsorships or through affiliate marketing.

Mike Wheeler is one of those capitalistic marketers cashing in on the Snuggie, literally, but it wasn't always that way. He created SnuggieSightings.com out of a fun idea at first, until the web site was mentioned in *USA Today*. "I built the site to have fun and be funny," he said. "When *USA Today* featured me, I hit the top of Google Trends that day, and did over 20,000 hits on my web site. It was a disaster. My webhost freaked out because of the traffic spike and shut down the server. Then some people who sell the Snuggie contacted me and told me about affiliate marketing and how I could make money from it. So I did, and it's great." Why is the Snuggie such a great seller for Mike? "It's the humor factor. It adds value to the content, and people want to share it. It's entertainment. Because people share it more easily, I don't have to do a lot to drive eyeballs to it, which makes it easily monetizeable. I could sell other things, but a Snuggie is cheap and fun, and a heck of a lot easier to sell than a Blu-Ray player."

In 2009, Mike made more money online than he did over at his day job, creating yet another believer in the cult of Internet marketing. "When I got that first check, I was amazed," said Mike. "I took a picture of it. I'll never forget it."

Mike's story is indicative of pretty much every self-made Internet marketer, and a good example of the power of fun. Too many people overlook fun when it comes to their business. Sure, you could be in the most boring industry in the world, such as insurance, but that shouldn't stop you from trying to add a little fun into your marketing.

My older brother, Kenneth Kukral, owns a specialty insurance underwriting firm called International Excess (Intlxs .com). As I mentioned, in my opinion, the insurance industry is dreadfully boring (sorry bro). So how do you find ways to draw attention to something that most people aren't really interested in? Well, International Excess has always been viewed as being on the cutting edge of creativity in the specialty risk industry. They differentiate themselves by "thinking outside the box" and coming up with unique solutions to risk opportunities.

Oftentimes opportunities for risk coverage, that have not been done before, present themselves. For example, a Government contractor was jobbed with putting up surveillance and monitoring equipment in, of all places, Guantanamo Bay, Cuba. As you can imagine, this kind of work is both highly unusual and most likely even dangerous. Most insurance companies wouldn't touch this type of risk with a ten-foot pole. International Excess was able to put together a package of general liability, contingent auto liability, accidental death and dismemberment coverage, and kidnap and extortion coverage on a 3-year policy that allowed the contractor to go in safely and begin work knowing that if something bad happened, they'd be covered.

It's creative and risk-taking thinking like this that allows International Excess to stand-out from their competitors, and allows them to continue to lead the way in their industry and create new revenue generating streams of business.

59

Luxury versus Need

IS WHAT YOU'RE selling a luxury or a need? There's a difference for sure. The Snuggie is one of those mega-selling hybrid items that could serve as both, but certainly most everything else falls under one or the other category. A luxury item is a product or service that customers *would like* to have. A need item is a product or service that, well, customers *need* to have. For example, water is a need item, but when you put it in a bottle and sell it for three bucks it then becomes a luxury item. Marketers ruin everything, don't they? That's a joke, sorta.

Seriously folks, start thinking about what you're selling and how your customers perceive it, because until you figure it out, you're never going to be able to sell that product to your target market. Ask yourself this question, "Can my customer live without this product?" If the answer is yes, you're selling a luxury item. If the answer is no, then you have a need. Once you have that figured out you can begin to build a marketing plan and start selling. Below are a few examples of need items versus luxury items. There's some extra space left over for you to add in your products or services. If you're not sure what you sell it might be time to ask your customers.

Need	Luxury
Anything with wheels to get me to work and the grocery store	Rolls Royce Phantom
Water	Bottled Water
Food	Morton's Steak Dinner
Shoes	Manolo Blahnik's
Money	A Billion Dollars
Air	Oxygen Bars

The difference between luxury and need is not always about price. Remember, your product or service is defined by how much pain it takes away from the customer. Pricing can vary in such circumstances. Luxury items are usually priced higher simply because they can, or because the quality of the item is made with higher-quality materials or by a famous brand. Need items are priced by the market of supply and demand. Milk at the grocery store or new tires for your car are good examples of need items that are priced by demand.

Vincent James is songwriter/musician who writes custom love songs at LoveSongs.com. You can order a love song for your loved one for a few hundred dollars. Maybe get one for your spouse on your anniversary. Order one as a wedding gift for an upcoming marriage for your cousin Ralphy. The beauty of the idea and the product is that it's a gift that is unlike any other. It won't break and it won't go away and you'll have it forever. The problem for Vincent is that his web site lacks a good marketing touch, actually making it hard to convince someone to buy the product. This is a great example of a luxury versus need item. Actually, this is more like a novelty item, *and* a luxury item, which makes it even harder to sell.

Another thing to remember is that the market can sometimes define your product. For example, in a recession, an item like Dunkin Donuts coffee can easily go from being a need item to a luxury item. Sure, you need it every morning and oh, how good it tastes, but when you have bills to pay and you've lost your job, it becomes something you can do without. In the business of Web consulting and coaching, the recession turned the luxury item of teaching you how to make a living online from being a luxury item to a need item. Follow the market and keep a close eye on what it is that you sell and how your customer perceives it, then plan, price, and market accordingly.

60

Getting Attention the Old-Fashioned Way

KEVIN SAVETZ IS owner of Savetz Publishing (SavetzPublishing .com). Kevin's 90+ web sites generate more than 8 million page views per month, and his FreePrintable.net newsletter has more than 250,000 subscribers. His web site FaxZero.com allows users to send faxes from their computers for free, and users have sent more than 2 million faxes since the web site's inception. Kevin has been online since the 1980s and started out as a computer journalist, writing several books about the Internet as well as thousands of articles on technology topics for publications including *Computer Shopper* and the *Washington Post*.

Get it? Kevin knows how to run and promote successful Web businesses. He calls himself an "Un-Marketer" with an old-fashioned style of promotion. Below is an interview and some tips Kevin provided:

Jim: You call yourself an "Un-Marketer." So you hate marketers, is that it?

Kevin: I am in many ways an affront to some of the more-recent takes on marketing. I went to journalism school and my stomach churns at the thought of deceptive, gimmicky, or poser marketing. I think "sell the story, not the product" usually only works with unintelligent or naïve consumers, and I'd rather have smart people who come back for my stuff again and again because it's good.

Jim: Does attention work?

Kevin: I've seen what happens when marketing is approached as a one-shot deal: You get a Digg spike or other form of attention with the result of short-term recognition but few ongoing sales or ad clicks. It could be argued that any attention is good attention, but I don't want drive-by gawkers; I want people who will stay because they like my product or service. There's no point in getting millions of people to check out my printables (business cards, stationery, calendars, coloring pages, etc.) if they're not top-quality or aren't what the visitor needs. They'd just look and leave.

Jim: Explain your old-fashioned marketing and pitching method.

Kevin: I take the classic "rifle approach" and pitch print (and other traditional) media, as well as bloggers, with a person-alized note that lets them know how your product/service/free items serve their readers as well as their editorial needs. I'm a soft-seller in a hard-sell world, and I believe that old-school philosophy, plus my quality product, is why I stand out to decision makers.

Jim: What are your top tips for someone who calls themself an "Un-Marketer"?

Kevin:

1. Make sure you don't get wrapped up in the flash and spin. Your ego likes attention but your pocketbook likes long-term, sustainable revenue based on people learning about and recognizing a quality product.

2. Don't overlook traditional approaches to marketing and PR. Many of these tried-and-true techniques still work but are being forgotten in the quest for short-term attention-getting strategies.

3. Take the time to direct your media (traditional or online) and pitch to the right person, by name. Take a couple of

minutes to Google or check LinkedIn and make sure the person you have in mind is still at the same publication, with the same contact information. (Don't rely on an old list or masthead; media jobs are like a revolving door right now.)

4. Know the publication or blog you're pitching so you don't waste your time or theirs. Mention specific sections of the newspaper or column, or the magazine you're pitching. Editors want to see that you've put some effort into knowing their publication and aren't sending exactly the same boilerplate to everyone.

5. Make it personal. Show editors/bloggers how your product or service helps them and their readers. What's in it for them? If you pitch the right editor or reporter at the right time, in the right context, ideally you will help them solve a problem or fill a gap in coverage and you're well on your way to getting the attention you crave.

6. Check publications' editorial calendars to make pitches even more appropriate. Pitch seasonal stuff three or four months in advance for print media and several weeks in advance to online editors. Suggest local angles or other possible angles (for example, your product could be part of a larger feature on an industry or trend). Don't try to sell a "bad fit."

7. And here's where I deviate from much of the new-school marketing that's going on today. Don't be pushy and definitely don't be condescending. There's not an editor on the planet who wants to hear, "You're missing out if you don't see why you need to run this," which is basically another way of calling them stupid.

8. Finally, be brief, say thanks, and be available and responsive when you do get that call.

61

Power to the People

SHEL HOROWITZ HAS been helping businesses, services, authors, publishers, and nonprofits with marketing for more than 30 years. The author of seven books (three of which won awards), he's an expert in frugal, ethical, and effective marketing, including major media publicity, social networking, powerful joint ventures, and much more. However, perhaps what Shel is the most proud of is his ability to help make meaningful change in the world through the development of grass-roots campaigns and organizations. Yes, with enough of the right kind of attention, you can be noticed, and change the world. It's not always about making money, thankfully.

You see, there was a beautiful mountaintop where Shel lived that was about to be developed into a residential zone. I guess so gazillionaires could build their gigantic mansions up there and look out over all the regular folk. Who knows the reason. The point is that nobody wanted it to happen except the gazillionaires and the developer standing to make their own pile of money. This was pristine, untouched land that shouldn't be ruined by man. What Shel did to save it was create an environmental organization called Save the Mountain. He knew the only way to stop this travesty was to make a big enough stink about it, because when you make a big stink about something, you're more likely to get noticed.

"All the experts issued variations on 'this is terrible, but there's nothing we can do.' That's when I got mad enough to not only start the group, but to donate several hundred hours of time writing and distributing press releases and position statements, doing media interviews and other public outreach, testifying at public hearings, and organizing," said Shel. "I had figured it would be a 5-year effort, but it was worth it to protect the neighborhood I had chosen to live out most of the rest of my life."

What happened was typical of most attention-getting efforts of this kind. Success! The first meeting for the organization had more than 70 people jammed into Shel's house. Those same people, under the Save the Mountain banner, worked to get more than 70 media stories in printed publications, as well as a few dozen radio and TV appearances. More than 1,000 people in the small town of only 5,000 helped the fight by at least a bumper sticker, petition, or lawn sign.

The results? The people won and defeated the supposedly invincible project in just 13 months. Why did it work? There's a critical piece to this story that needs to be recognized. Sure, the people were mad as hell and they were vocal about it, but what really turned up the most heat on the project was the massive attention from the media. Politicians, rich people, and elected officials in general have been getting away with murder for years because most of the time they're never put under any *real* pressure. A lot of media attention changes all that, and fast.

Since most people aren't public relations gurus or marketing people, they fail to realize that you have to make a story out of your campaign in order for the media to latch onto it. The story also has to be good. You can't just walk into a reporter's office without doing your research or having a prepared pitch in place. They don't really care about your goal, the same way they don't give a you-know-what about your business if that's what you're pitching. The media wants a story. The want something juicy to give to their audience. They make money by getting as many readers/viewers/listeners as they can, and without something good to give to their customers, they will lose their jobs.

The second thing to mention about the significance of this campaign is that crowds matter. Would Shel have had as much success if it were an organization of him, his wife, and his neighbor only? Most likely not. Three people does not a story make, while 70 people and $\frac{1}{5}$ of the town does.

62

One "Hell" of an Attention-Getter

RANDY CASSINGHAM IS a master at getting attention. His *This Is True* newsletter, established in 1994, is one of the first for-profit Internet newsletters. In 1994 just the concept of something fun to do on the fledgling Internet got him lots of press attention, including not just computer publications but also *Newsweek*, the *New York Times*, the *Los Angeles Times, Playboy,* and more. With more than 100,000 subscribers to the weekly newsletter, his business is still going strong today.

With a significant percentage of e-mail addresses going bad every week, it takes a sustained effort to get the attention needed to keep new newsletter subscribers coming in week after week to have a successful e-mail campaign. For Randy, one attention-getting promotional idea not only went viral, it turned out to be a significant source of income.

It started in 2000, when a reader told Randy that he was going to hell for a story he wrote—it was an "anti-Christian" story, the reader claimed. When Randy tried to reason with her by saying a minister had no problem with the story, she said he was going to hell too! It was crazy, but it gave Randy a great idea: For his response he created a Get Out of Hell Free® card, a parody of the

251

Get Out of Jail Free card included in Monopoly® games. He calls them the "GOOHF" card for short—pronounced "goof," of course!

He then told his newsletter readers the story about how he was condemned to hell by one of their fellow readers, and of course described his solution to the problem: his Get Out of Hell Free card. He told readers that if they're tired of nosy people telling them what to think or how to believe, he would send them 10 cards for a dollar—the cost of printing, packing, and postage.

Readers responded immediately and orders streamed in, and have continued at a strong pace since. They don't just want 10 cards, though; the average order is for 150 cards, with many ordering boxes of them. Of course, every card has Randy's URL on it, so every card given out means someone new finds out about Randy's web site and newsletter. Because the card is so fun, people tend to keep them or pass them on, rather than throw them away. To keep up with demand, Randy has 60,000 cards printed at a time.

The resulting attention is significant: The total sales to date have exceeded 1.4 million cards—and that doesn't count the hundreds of t-shirts, hundreds of thousands of stickers, hundreds of coffee mugs, and countless other "GOOHF" trinkets, many of which are issued as limited edition items. He set up a web site, GetOutofHellFree.com, to both sell the cards and trinkets, and help bring attention back to his bread-and-butter flagship site, ThisIsTrue.com.

Thousands of people from dozens of countries have purchased the cards with Randy's web site prominently mentioned for the explicit purpose of giving them away to others. That would be pretty powerful even if Randy were giving away all those cards as an advertising effort. Instead people are buying them, and in such quantity that instead of breaking even as Randy intended, the cards and, over time, the many related products, have turned into a significant profit center themselves.

Meanwhile, people *constantly* mention the card in the "Where did you hear about us?" box when they subscribe to This Is True, Randy told me in an interview for this book.

Few find the card offensive. Randy says ministers are among his best customers, and there are even two priests posted to the Vatican who carry them! One priest even has a GOOHF t-shirt that he sometimes wears under his cassock. Readers send him stories, which he posts on the GOOHF web site. One tells the story of a woman who slipped a card into her grandfather's coat pocket before the funeral director closed his coffin.

His readers have lots of fun handing out the cards to friends, harried waitresses, overworked retail clerks, cops that let them go without giving them a ticket—anyone who needs a little reward or smile. Best of all, well more than 1 million people have been exposed to Randy's web site through the cards, bringing countless thousands of new subscribers to his newsletter, and that attention will continue for years to come.

Nevertheless, a word of warning: such a tactic is not for the faint-hearted. Hasbro, which owns the Monopoly® board game, did object to the cards, which meant Randy had to hire a lawyer to fight back with his parody defense. For Randy, that was worth it, especially since it worked. Therefore, 1.4 million cards (and counting) later, Randy has a new trademarked brand, a significant side business, and a killer word-of-mouth attention-getting promotion that runs constantly. Moreover, he has something that any business would love: a negative advertising budget!

63

Astonish Me!

Since 1997, Leo J Quinn, Jr., has been teaching thousands of people in bad financial trouble how to improve their financial situation. No stranger to getting attention, Leo has used things like baby bottles, bank bags, frisbees, and even rubber balls to get in front of new customers. At conferences, you will likely see him walking around with a scrolling digital name tag.

As most great marketers like Leo know, if you can get a potential customer on the phone you have a much better chance of closing them. So how do you get a potential client to pay attention to you and actually pick up the phone and call you? E-mails work, sure, but anyone who has ever done e-mail marketing knows that only a small percentage of recipients respond to e-mail solicitations, especially if you are selling to them over and over again. That's why Leo decided to get creative and try something different. Here's his story:

> I had just finished reading a book that gave me some advice that hit me right between the eyes. Just two words: ASTONISH ME! Those two simple words really got my brain churning

on how I could astonish my potential customers. I thought to myself, "What would astonish me?" Then one day as I walking through Wal-Mart it hit me.

What would you think if someone sent you a cell phone in the mail? It would astonish me. At the very least, I'd be super-curious and want to investigate it further. So I did some research and found out I could get pre-paid cell phones for about $20 that come with about 20-minutes of talk time built in after registration. The idea was that I would spend a small amount of money on cell phones and send them out in the mail to my best leads. Of course, I pre-programmed them with my phone number first, and I included a one-page letter explaining what this was all about and showing them how to call me.

I chose ten potential leads and mailed the phone and letter out in a U.S. Priority Mail box. The postage was $4.05 per box since it was under one pound, bringing my total out of pocket cost to just under $25 per lead, so in total I spent about $277 (taxes) total to test this idea.

I wasn't sure what was going to happen. Would anyone call? One thing was for sure, I'd find out in a few days. As each package arrived, the phone calls started coming in, all from excited and astonished people who just couldn't believe what I had sent them.

They just had to call me they all said. Of course, when it was actually me on the other end of the phone they were equally astonished.

Overall, the test worked. I spent $277 and made $5,903 in sales from it. Not a bad return on investment.

What Leo found out is that attention does in fact equal revenue. Following is the content of the one-page letter included in the package.

Dear {NAME}

As you can see I've included a real live working telephone with this mailing.

Why have I done this? Two reasons:

1. I needed a way to be sure I got your attention.
2. I wanted to make it as easy as possible for you to get in touch with me.

Enclosed you will find information about and a copy of my "How to Own Your Paycheck Again" program. This shows people how to pay off their debt in a fraction of the normal time.

Since 1997, I have been providing this information to people in classes throughout NY, NJ, and MA. In 2001, I started making this information available on my web site as a downloadable program.

I've been on your mailing list for a time and I notice that you do endorse products to your subscribers.

As you can see from the enclosed material, I have affiliates in just about every niche you can imagine. Regardless of their other interests most people have credit card debt alongside mortgages and car loans.

Please take a few moments to review the program and then hit SEND on the cell phone. My telephone number is already programmed in, the phone is on and ready to go.

Thank you very much.

Sincerely,

Leo Quinn

64

Does Making S#*% Up to Get Attention Work?

SURE IT DOES, it happens all the time. A town in Israel is claiming a mermaid shows up at night to frolic in the sea for all those that want to watch. Local officials are now offering a cash prize of $1 million for the first tourist to take a photograph of the mermaid. Look, we all know there is no mermaid, so nobody is going to make the million bucks, despite what "the town's people say." What's more likely: That there is a real mermaid or that the local tourism board or a politician made up the story to drive tourists to visit their town? What happens when you have tourists? They spend money on food, beverages, lodging, and merchandise. Once again, attention equals revenue.

How many millions of people have visited Loch Ness in Scotland to try to catch a glimpse of the legendary Nessie, the Loch Ness Monster? How much money have people made off tracking down Bigfoot, or the lost city of Atlantis? How many historical societies have claimed ghost hauntings to get more people through the doors? How many people have flown to Area

51 in Roswell, Nevada, to see for themselves if aliens do in fact exist?

The answer to the previous questions is a lot. More than you can count, and they're all customers.

From the time when each of us was a little child we've been told stories, and usually the best ones are the ones we remember the longest. Books, movies, radio programs, and so on, and now on the Web. There's an opportunity for you to tap into those feelings we all had as a child, of being wide-eyed and excited, sitting there wondering how the story is going to end. Your customers want that from you and they crave it.

There's no reason you can't make something up to get attention for your business. Your customers might like a nice ghost story. No, you don't have to create a monster who writes your blog or pretend there's a ghost in your copy machine. Forget monsters and ghosts. The point is that making things up sometimes just works. And no, this isn't making up lies to deceive. Consider a made up idea to be marketing, because that's part of what good marketing is. It is just telling stories. All marketers do this in some way or another. The difference between the good marketers and the bad ones is that the good marketers embellish and create to help make you aware of a need, and the bad ones are just trying to deceive you.

Your potential customer is looking for something from you that they can latch onto, and telling a story is a great way to give it to them. I'm not talking about having a robust "about us" page on your web site (which is important to have, yes). I'm talking about creating a story out of your brand/product/service/team, and so on. . . . What is unique, different, fun, sad, or amazing about how your business or career came about? Tell that story, and if you don't have one, create one.

Storytelling is an art in many ways, but it can be an art that is learned. Successful copywriters are master storytellers. They are able to tap into the emotions of their readers, engaging them, and leading them to an eventual ending. In the world of marketing, that is the call to action.

65

The Best Job in the World

THERE ARE THOUSANDS and thousands of beautiful tropical and exotic locations to travel to around the globe. Millions of people travel the globe annually spending obscene amounts of money to stay in the most exclusive locations. I love living in Cleveland, Ohio, but let's face it, when I am looking for a place to go on vacation I usually look for a place with endless blue skies, crystal clear bath warm water, and fancy umbrella drinks. A swim-up pool bar is a bonus.

Like you, the hardest part is figuring out where to go. There are too many decisions you need to make. So what do we do? We go to Google and do a search, or we call a travel agent (yes, they still exist), or more than likely we take recommendations from friends or associates about the last amazing place they went to. Still though, it's a tough call. That's why tourism bureaus exist. Their job is to find creative ways to get the word out about why we should come to visit them . . . and spend our hard-earned money.

Did you ever hear of the Queensland Islands on the Great Barrier Reef? Neither did I, until they broke through in 2009 with one of the most creative and talked about publicity campaigns ever achieved by a tourism bureau. The story was brilliant and the execution flawless. They created a new job for the island called "caretaker" and branded it as "The Best Job in the World." Then they opened up the application process to anyone in the world. All you had to do was prepare a short video about why you wanted the job. Of course, the most creative video and worthy person would win the job and get to spend six months exploring the Islands of the Great Barrier Reef while reporting on his/her travels through regular blog posts.

More than 34,000 people from around the globe, in almost every country known, applied for the opportunity to win the job. Of course, because it was called The Best Job in the World, the media latched onto the story like you wouldn't believe. Therefore, not only did the tourism bureau of Queensland get more than 34,000 videos promoting their location, they also got thousands and thousands of media stories from major news outlets and bloggers alike.

Ben Southall of Britain eventually won the job and spent 6 months frolicking the islands on jet skis, wrestling with jellyfish, getting a great tan, and, of course, making a name for himself and a new popular tourist location for them. Sure, they could have spent a few million dollars on advertising to get the word out, but don't you agree that this attention-getting idea was a far better idea?

66

Porn and Pancakes at Church

How DO YOU get more people to church? The answer, porn and pancakes, of course. A church in Southbrook, near Dayton, Ohio, offers a breakfast where you can come and learn about the dangers of porn addiction. Of course, there wasn't going to be any porn shown at the breakfast, but you could certainly get quite a bit of attention with the title. File this one under "we shouldn't really do that, should we?" category. Yes, you should.

Sometimes you need to embrace your inner troublemaker and do things that you know might ruffle a few feathers if you want to get noticed and reach a goal. How hard of a sell do you think it was for the organizers at that church in Dayton to convince their longest and most virtuous members on the idea of porn and pancakes? Who was the woman who stood up in the meeting and floated that idea? Do you think that took courage? Usually the best ideas are the ones that make half the room laugh and the other half gasp in disgust or terror. That's how you know when you have a great idea, an idea that is going to get noticed.

Speaking of pancakes, Sean O'Connor thought there had to be an easier way to make pancakes. Millions of people around the world enjoy pancakes every day, and we all know what a big pain in the butt it is to have to make the batter first, then fry the pancakes, and then clean it up. It's time consuming, messy, and, well, it's an inconvenience, but oh, the pancakes are so good and we must still have them. That's why Sean created Batter Blaster, an organic pancake and waffle mix that comes in a pressurized can, complete with a point and shoot nozzle, just like a whip-cream can.

Fifteen-million dollars later, Sean's product now appears in more than 15,000 outlets nationwide, including Whole Foods, Costco, and, by the time of this book's publication, Wal-Mart. However, Sean knew that just because he had a unique idea it did not mean he was going to be able to sell it. It was going to take something extra. That's when Sean decided to take matters into his own hands and get his product into the hands of consumers he knew would love it, who would then demand it from their retail outlets.

"We had to go nonconventional with our marketing, because we couldn't afford 'regular' marketing," said O'Connor. "So we took it to the street, setting up impromptu stands on New York City street corners where we cooked pancakes and handed them out, until the police came and asked for our permits. We traveled 180,000 miles in an Airstream trailer to visit county fairs; rallying a team to cook 76,382 pancakes in 8 hours to set a Guinness World Record."

What Sean had to do was change consumer behavior. "People were used to the way they had been doing it forever," he said. "Once we put it into their hands and showed them how it worked they were able to visualize it, and that's when they were more able to accept the change in behavior."

67

The Worst Is Sometimes Better Than the Best

ANYONE CAN MAKE a list of the best things, but it's the people who have the guts to make a list of the worst things that get attention. Richard Blackwell became a cultural icon during his career after creating the "Worst Dressed List," where he mercilessly panned celebrities for what they were wearing. Today that flag continues to wave in the hands of people such as Perez Hilton and before him *People Magazine*, Joan Rivers, and the E! cable TV channel. It's really become a business.

Creating bad attention can be good and the opportunity for you is immense. While everyone in your niche is out there creating content about the best things, you could be doing the exact opposite and talking about the worst things. They zig, you zag, and you get more attention.

If you're a plumber, make a list of the stupidest and worst things dumb plumbers do to screw up a job, then send it out to your customers for a laugh and ask them to give it to a friend. If you're a consultant, write an eBook talking about how to not get ripped off from consultants, then give it away free online so you get maximum downloads and reads. If you're a Web designer, feature the top 100 worst designed corporate web sites, and how they could fix them, then take your list and post it on your blog. Then send out a press release about it linking back to your blog. Update the blog post into your Facebook page, and tell all your Twitter followers about it and ask them to retweet it.

68

Five Cents Is More Memorable Than Free

WHEN TIMES ARE tough and work is scarce, we all need to find ways to stand out from the crowd. After being laid off from an architecture firm for the second time, John Morefield knew something had to change. He could look for another job again, or give it a go on his own once and for all. So what did he do to get customers? He set up a booth at a local market in Seattle, Washington, and offered home renovation advice for five cents a shot. That's right, five cents.

Every Sunday, Morefield goes down to this local market and sets up a small table usually in between the guy selling fresh fish and the gal selling organic vegetables. He's there to offer expert advice on things like remodeling your kitchen or how best to add that second floor to your home. Of course, it's only 5 cents for his advice, which customers are expected to drop into a jar sitting on the tabletop. Silly, yes, but it works. He's gotten many customers to hire him to do things like review the plans for their remodel job, or even get him to come up with his own plans for what he would do. He's now well on his way to building a clientele that will ensure he never has to look for another job again.

Why not just go free? Well, free is great, but 5 cents is memorable and gets your attention. Here's an idea: Try pricing your products or services differently to get noticed. Why not make up a fake product and price it at some outrageous price like $10 million dollars? Put it on your sell sheet of offerings and pitch it to your customers during sales meetings. Add some funny features to the product like having the CEO of your firm coming to their house and shoveling snow for them, or throw in a Ferrari and ownership of their own private island.

Write this one up as another one of those "can we do that?" moments. A car dealership in Chicago is offering you a car for $1 when you buy one at regular price. Yep, if you come in and buy a new Chrysler Pacifica, you can drive away with a Chrysler PT Cruiser for only one buck! Sounds like a great way to get some customers into your show floor, and that it did, generating free media exposure and, of course, sales. Promotions like this work so well because they make the customer, and the media, turn their head in your direction.

69

Sometimes It's the Little Ideas That Work Best

SOMETIMES STANDING UP on a chair in a room and screaming at the top of your lungs does in fact work when you want to get someone's attention. You may not realize it, but you've most likely done something in your life to get attention in that manner, even in some small way, but probably not as loud. The point is attention getting is not always about landing that big client or getting your own reality TV show. We all understand that to get what we want we sometimes have to speak up and take matters into our own hands. Following are a few stories from some people who did exactly that.

Ari J. Greenberg was trying to get the attention of a bigwig at the number-one apartment web site in the country. "I could never get the guy on the phone and he never responded to my e-mails," said Ari. "So I decided to send two dozen bagels and cream cheese to his office one morning with a note that read, "Dear Mike, I hope your team enjoys the breakfast. Best, Ari." Did it work? "This definitely got his attention. I received a call that day (his team enjoyed the bagels) and we signed a partnership agreement."

Tom Rice couldn't get his contractor who was fixing up his house to show up and work, or answer his phone calls and e-mails. "I gave him an ultimatum to contact me by a certain day, or something truly embarrassing was going to occur," said Tom. "He did not decide to answer by the appropriate day or time, so I called up the local newspaper and placed an ad in the lost and found column, like he was a pet: *Lost: My builder. Answers to the name of Bob. If you see him, please tell him to finish my house. —Tom Rice"* Of course, the real ad had the real name of the builder in it.

Did it work? The next day Tom had five builders working on his house, who then completed it in record time. "In my case, my ad was directed towards one specific individual, and yeah, it was worth every bit of the 10 bucks I spent."

Darren Bryant couldn't get anyone from Bank of America to pay attention to him and answer his questions. He was spending hours in what he calls Bank of America's "phone maze," getting bounced from person to person, never reaching somebody who could address his situation. That was until he created a five-minute video explaining his troubles and uploaded it to You-Tube. The video included his phone number and e-mail address. He then e-mailed it to over a dozen Bank of America e-mail addresses he found online. Four hours later Bryant got a phone call from somebody at the bank asking for his account number and promising to forward it to someone who would investigate his situation.

Ann Minch went viral with a video she posted on YouTube where she proclaimed she wouldn't pay off her credit card debt unless the "evil, thieving bastards" at Bank of America lowered her interest rate. Within a week of its posting an executive got in touch with Minch and agreed to her demand. After that, it seems that other Bank of America customers hopped onboard as well, creating dozens of videos with some of the same problems, creating a firestorm for the bank, and tarnishing their brand.

70

Stalker or Author? Who Cares? It Worked!

THERE'S A FINE line between a restraining order and being very passionate when trying to get attention. Camille McConnell wanted to get her new book, called *Stop Overeating Today!*, featured on the internationally popular Dr. Laura radio program as Book of the Week. There was one big problem. All attempts at contacting Dr. Laura the traditional ways weren't working. That's when Camille decided to try a different way to get attention. She wrapped up a copy of her book in a bubble envelope with a thick coating of pink sparkles (Dr. Laura's favorite color), glued sequins on the envelope in the shape of her logo, and sent it out. Guess what happened? No response. It didn't work, but Camille didn't give up. This time she sent Dr. Laura another book, this time in a bright pink envelope, with a picture of Dr. Laura she found online, along with a cartoon-like bubble coming out of her mouth saying, "this is a really good book!"

Now, at this point two things could have happened. The first could have been that the producers at the Dr. Laura show could have filed a restraining order on the "crazy lady who keeps sending weirdly wrapped and colorful packages with cut-outs of Dr. Laura on them." Or, they could have picked up the phone, called her, and booked her for the show. Fortunately, for Camille, they decided to go for the latter. "That finally got her attention, and because of my persistence my book did in fact get featured on her show, helping me sell a ton of books in one day and helping me get ranked by Amazon as a top selling book in the extremely competitive diet/weight loss category," said McConnell.

71

An Idea Turned into Millions!

PETE WILLIAM OFTEN gets called the Australian version of billionaire Sir Richard Branson. This is not because he also has a few billion dollars lying around, but more likely because he is a smart entrepreneur and businessman with a knack for making money and getting attention. Pete is most famous for working out a scheme to sell Australia's version of Yankee Stadium, The Melbourne Cricket Ground when he was only 21-years-old. Here's his story.

Back when I was 21, I sold Australia's version of Yankee Stadium—The Melbourne Cricket Ground for $500 and got national media exposure. I was reading the book, *The One Minute Millionaire*, and in it, it tells the story of a guy from New Jersey, who in the 1980s sold old pieces of the famous Brooklyn Bridge's walkway timber. He went about creating 5" × 11" certificates outlining the history of the bridge, attaching a small piece of the timber and selling them for around $14.95 each, and word around the campfire is that he made like $2 million from it.

Obviously as a young Trump-wanna-be I loved this idea, and started to think how I could rip this idea off, replicate the idea, and implement it here in Australia. It was a much better idea then pinching golf balls off the local pitch-n-putt to resell. After racking the brain for about 10 minutes, I realized the Melbourne Cricket Ground was under reconstruction and the Ponsford Stand had just been ripped down. On the back of a few phone calls and newly found entrepreneurial-confidence, I was able to track down the wrecking company that was demolishing the Ponsford stand, who said they had a significant amount of timber from the seating and flooring as hoped. However, to my amazement they also had a considerable amount of the world famous MCC Crested Carpet—which originally lay in the members dining room. So after rushing down the highway the following morning to view the magnificent carpet just lying in the corner of the wreckers' warehouse I took all the remaining crested carpet, along with a mass of timber.

From that point on I enlisted the help of some friends who helped create a series of framed limited edition sports memorabilia pieces that sold from $595 to $1,495. These included a photo of the structure, a piece of the famous carpet and even a limited number series that had their frame created out of the timber that was once the stadium. Amongst a wide range of creative and unique marketing techniques and strategies employed, a press release created with the headline "21-Year-Old Sells MCG for Under $500" generated over $50,000 of FREE advertising and publicity in media via Channel 7 news, *Herald Sun* articles, AM and FM Radio interviews, and trade magazine articles, which generated a huge proportion of sales at no cost. It was during all this free publicity that I was first referred to as "Australia's Richard Branson" by a member of the media, and it stuck.

Now just a few years later, Pete has begun to build his empire and be truly recognized as one of Australia's leading entrepreneurs, having been featured in almost every Australian business magazine including *The Bulletin, Money Magazine, Australian*

Anthill, Success Magazine, and many many more. "I was just awarded Global runner-up in JCI's Creative Young Entrepreneur of the Year Awards for 2009," he said. "I also wrote a book for Wiley Australia a few years back titled *How to Turn Your Million Dollar Idea into a Reality.*"

Conclusion
This Book Was Written for You

How do you feel right now? Have I done my job? I hope your brain is buzzing with a million ideas you can begin to put in motion to improve your business or build your brand. I hope you're ready to storm into tomorrow with a newfound excitement for finding ways to stand out and get attention.

I hope you're ready to run through a wall right now. Are you? That was my intent.

Like you, I have always found inspiration in how others before me have found success. This book was written for you, for that exact purpose: To educate you to see the possibilities that sit before you at this very moment; to help you understand that there are millions to be made, online and off, by taking chances and thinking in new, creative ways.

But more importantly, I wrote this book to inspire and motivate you to get off your behind and get something done. If there's one thing you should take away from reading this book, it's that the doers in life and business get what they want, and everyone else gets what they get. An entire new world awaits you if you're a doer. Everyone else, well, they choose to take what comes to them. They choose to worry about their egos or worry about failure, so much so it stops them from finding success.

That's not you. You know it's not. I know it and you know it. Like I said, I wrote this book for you. . . .

Now it's your turn. Where will you go from here? What will you do that is remarkable? How will you change your life or career? How will you stand out and get noticed and turn attention into revenue?

I'm excited to see what you come up with. Thank you for reading.

Please visit AttentiontheBook.com for tools, tips, tricks, free stuff (and fun).

But Wait . . . There's More!

Here is an offer for you. Schedule some free time with me by visiting www.connectwithjim.com. I'll get on the phone with you and we'll talk about your business and goals and see if I can come up with an attention-getting idea that you can use to skyrocket your sales, create a flood of referrals, and powder keg your publicity. What do you have to lose? It's free.

Index

5DayBootcamp.com, 132
The $7.95 Marketing Plan, 144
9/11, social media and, 15
10GoldenRules.com, 11
"21 Accents," 169
99designs.com, 219
500Words.com, 206
1938media.com, 11

ABC News, 222
Abestweb.com, 146
Ad Hustler, 75
The Adsense Code, 207
Affiliate Marketing, 10, 145–147
Affiliate Summit, 10, 12, 118, 147, 163
Alliteration, branding and, 77–78
Amazon.com, 64, 270
  S3 storage, 193
Amember.com, 144
Amway, 155
American Academy of Dramatic Arts, 71

Amyotrophic Lateral Sclerosis, 163
Anderson, Pamela, 215
Animoto.com, 193
Apologies, avoiding, 7
Apple, 18–19
Arenas, Gilbert, 227
Armstrong, Lance, 71
Askdavetaylor.com, 79, 218
"Askaninja," 170
AsktheBuilder.com, 79, 81
Associated Press (AP), 27, 55
Atlantic Records, 168
Attention, negative, 214–216
Australian Anthill, 273
Authenticity, 200
Aviva LLC, 74
Avon Walk for Breast Cancer, 163
AwesomeMillion.com, 63

Balloon Boy, 226
Bank of America, 48, 268
Banking, social media and, 14–15
Barefoot Executive, 143

BBC News, 222
Beaches & Cream Soda Shop, 211
BeautifulPeople.com, 228
Ben Folds, 167
Benefits, pitches and potential, 33
Berkowitz, Jay, 11, 138
Best Buy, 189
Bezos, Jeff, 64
Biden, Joe, 226
Big Mouth Billy, 236
Big Texan Steak Ranch, 210
BigBrownBox.com, 63
Bing, 230
Biscuit Hole campaign, 212
Biz Web Coach, 75, 134–135
Black Enterprise, 55
BlendTec, 153, 180–186
Blip.tv, 192–193
Blogging
   affiliate mark, 147
   branding and, 16
   free services and, 103
   subscribers as revenue, 2
   video, 154
Blogher, 20–21
Blogkits, 42
Blogmaverick.com, 39
Blogs to Riches, 16
Blogworld Expo, 42
Blu-Ray player, 240
BMW, 169
Boedecker, George B., Jr., 236
Bonuses, 139
Boot camps, 132–133
Branding
   building, 81–84
   nametags and, 8–9
   tips for, 76–80

Brandweek, 190
Branson, Richard, 20, 271
Bratton, Susan, 11
Brick Lane Curry House, 211
Brogan, Chris, 10, 12, 114
Brokaw, Tom, 72
Brooklyn Bridge, 44–45
Bryant, Darren, 48, 268
Buckley, Michael, 167
The Bulletin, 272
Burger King, 213

Call to action, pitches and,
   33–34
Can We Do That? Outrageous PR
   Stunts That Work—and Why
   Your Company Needs Them, 35
Caricatures, 218–219
Carroll, Teddy, 58
Carson, Johnny, 44, 45
Carter, Tim, 79, 81–84
Carvel ice cream, 34
Cassingham, Randy, 251–253
Causes on Facebook, 164
CBS, 232
CD continuity program, 130–131
Celebrity, 229
Celebrity Chatter, 167
Change, overcoming fear of, 24
Channel 3 (WKYC), 28
Charleston RiverDogs, 67, 68
Cheney, Dick, 31
Chicago Tribune, 223
Chicken Soup for the Soul, 70
Cho, Margaret, 232
Choices, confusion of too many,
   100–101
Christopher Reeve Foundation, 71

Chrysler, 266

Clark, Brian, 118

Clegg, Gary, 234

Cleveland Browns, 26

Cleveland LinkedIn Networking Group, 154

CNBC, 178–179

CNN, 44, 55, 227

CNN Money, 205

Coca-Cola, 182

Collins, Shawn, 10, 12, 118

Comcast, 151, 153

Comm, Joel, 10, 205–207

CommissionJunction.com, 146

Communication
  personalizing, 87–89
  See also Voice, having a

Community, subscribers and, 136–137

Computer Shopper, 245

Conference, speaking engagements as revenue, 2

Connor, James, 86

Consulting, free, 103

Conte, Jack, 168

Content Management Solutions (CMS), 36

Content, reusing, 138

Continuity programs, 130–131

Controversy, 261–262

Copyblogger.com, 118

Copycats, 234–236

The Corner Bar, 210–211

Cost per click (CPC), 171

Coupon Mom, 75

Coupons, 102

Courage, 260–261

Craigslist, 21

Creative Young Entrepreneur of the Year Award, 273

Credibility, pitches and, 33

Crocs, 236

Crossfit Cleveland, 172–173

Crowdspring.com, 219

The Crown Candy Kitchen, 210

Cruikshank, Lucas, 168

Cuban, Mark, 39–43

Customer evangelists, 237–241. *See also* Testimonials

Dahl, Gary, 235

Dallas Mavericks, 39

Dallas Morning News, 41

Database Diva, 74

The DaVinci Code, 207

Dawn, Nataly, 168

Daymude, Colin, 161–162

Deadlines, setting, 113

DeBeers, 66

Dell, 153

de los Santos, Manuel, 71

Demonstrations, online video, 190

Denger, Ginette, 58

Denny's, 212

Denny's Beer Barrel Pub, 210

Des Jardins, Jory, 20

Determination, 81–84

Dickson, Tom, 181, 183, 184

Digg, 246

Diligence, 81–84

The Dip, 49

Discipline, 81–84

Discounts, 102

Discovery Channel, 185, 186

Distractions, productivity and, 113

Domain name, 144

Domino's Pizza, 227
Don't Worry, Be Happy, 236
Donaldson, Sam, 72
DontheIdeaGuy.com, 60
Doubt, ending, 112
Dress, image and, 218
Duct Tape, 69
Dunkin Donuts, 243–244
DVD continuity program, 130–131

E!, 222, 263
eBook, 16, 144
Eliason, Frank, 151
Ellen, 17
E-mail, revenue and sign-ups, 2
Emanuel, Rahm, 226
Encyclopedia Britannica, 145
Enron Night, 68
Environmental organizations,
    248–249
Evening News with Katie Couric, 34
Evernote, 57
The Evolution of Dance, 169–170
Extraordinary, becoming, 114

Facebook
  branding and, 15
  employment, 157–160
  friends as revenue, 2
  generating ideas, 57–58
  image and, 218
  raising awareness, 161–164
  social and financial equity, 14
Failure, fear of, 115
Fame, 229
FancyFastFood.com, 62
FanProtest.com, 27
FaxZero.com, 245

Federal Trade Commission, 147
FedEx, 69
Feedback, internet marketing and
    sales, 90
FeedFront Magazine, 163
Feldman, Loren, 11, 12
Feldman, Lori, 74
Figglehorn, Fred, 168
Five Hour Energy drink, 94
Flip video camera, 177, 188
Food challenges, 208–211
Forbes, 44, 190
FourSquare & Gowalla, 156
The Franchise King, 73, 75, 118,
    220
Free Money to Change Your Life,
    197
Free Money to Pay Your Bills,
    197
Free, services, popularity of,
    102–103
FreePrintable.net, 245
Frey, James, 225
Fun Is Good, 67
Funnel, sales. *See* Sales, funnel

Geek Factory, 37
GeekCast.fm, 163
Get Out of Hell Free cards,
    251–253
Ginsberg, Scott, 8–9, 73
Gmail, 58
Goals
  short-term, 117–121
  See also Revenue, goals
Godaddy.com, 27
Godin, Seth, 10, 49
Goldman Sachs, 64

Google
  Adsense, 206–207
  Analytics, 99, 159
  News, 77
  Notebook, 58
  parallels to traditional media,
    31–32
  problem solving, 94
  simplicity of, 98–99
  Trends, 239
  universal search, 173–174
Grasshopper.com, 233
Green Business Owner, 143
Green, Al, 236
Greenberg, Ari J., 267
Gretzky, Wayne, 64, 231
Group coaching, 134–135

Hardee's, 212
Harding, Tonya, 67
HarperCollins, 158, 159, 160
Hartunian, Paul, 44–45
Harvey, Paul, 44
Hasbro, 253
"Hastily Made Cleveland Tourism
  Video," 169
HBO, 168
Headshots, 218
hellomynameisscott.com, 9
Helpareporter.com (HARO), 10,
  35–37
Herald Sun, 272
Hilton, Paris, 78, 215
Hilton, Perez, 263
Hintze, Robert, 228
Hirepasha.com, 223
History Channel, 185
Hoffman, Brandon, 57

Home Depot, 189
Hook, determining the, 73–75
Horowitz, Shel, 248–249
Horsepigcow.com, 11
Houston Chronicle, 55
*How to Turn Your Million Dollar Idea
  into a Reality*, 273
Howes, Lewis, 11, 16–17, 154
Hsieh, Tony, 128
Hunt, Tara, 11
HyperText Markup Language
  (HTML), 219
Hypertext Preprocessor (PHP), 144

IdeaLady.com, 55
Ideas, generating, 51–59, 60–61
  free services, 103
iFart application, 10, 205–207
Image, 217–219
Inc., 190
International Excess, 240
Internet
  reasons people use the, 91–92
  sales environment, 98–106
*Interview Tactics! How to Survive the
  Media without Getting
  Clobbered!*, 222
iPhone
  branding and, 80
  generating ideas and, 57
iPod, 19
iTunes, 19, 206
IwearYourShirt.com, 63

James, Vincent, 243
JetBlue Airways, 20, 153
Jobs, Steve, 18
JoeBees, 238

Johnson, Bob, 71
Johnston, Levi, 227
Jones Soda, 21–25

Kirk, Harvey, 72
The Kitchen Sink, 211
Kitsch, 235
Kownacki, Justin, 231–232
Kukral, Kenneth, 240
Kurko, Jane Velz, 57

Laipply, Judson, 169–170
Larry King, 198
Late Night with Conan O'Brien, 17
Late Night with David Letterman, 198
Lauren, Ralph, 64
Law & Order, 20
Lee, Ryan, 140–141
Lesko, Matthew, 10, 197–201, 215
Libava, Joel, 73, 118, 220
LinkedIn, 11, 153
    connections as revenue, 2
    image and, 218
LIVESTRONG Foundation, 163
Logo, 219
Los Angeles Times, 251
LoveSongs.com, 243
Luxury, vs. need, 242–244

MacDonald, Kyle, 63
Madison, Ashley, 228
Magnolia Pictures, 42
"Man in the Box," 168–169
Man vs. Food, 209
Manolo Blahnik, 243
Marketing
    internet, 85–92
    outrageous, 65–69

Marketing Outrageously, 69
Mary Kay, 155
Mashable, 19, 205
Mays, Billy, 10, 12, 139
McConnell, Camille, 269–270
McDonald's, 182
McFerrin, Bobby, 236
Me 2.0, 78
"The Mean Kitty Song," 168
Media, trending topics, 27
Megale, Megan, 34
Melbourne Cricket Ground, 271
Membergate, 142–143
Membership, web sites, 124–129
Membership Site Owner, 143
Metallica, 53
MichRX Consulting Services, 143
Microsoft, 128
Million Dollar Homepage, 63
A Million Little Pieces, 225
Minch, Ann, 268
Mona Lisa, 235
Money, 44, 272
Monopoly, 252, 253
Morecalled Memo, 58
Morefield, John, 265
Morning Coach, 75
Morton's Steak, 243
Moye, David, 178–179
Mozart, Wolfgang Amadeus, 53
MSN, 230
Murphy, Gayl, 222
Murphy, Ted, 11
Murray, Bill, 68

Naddaff, George, 212
The NASCAR Cafe', 211
Nasol, Rico, 187

National Basketball Association (NBA), 39, 227
National Breast Cancer Foundation, 163
National Public Radio, 179
NBC, 205, 223
Need, vs. luxury, 242–244
Negativity, 115
Netflix.com, 127
New Jersey Monthly, 44
New York Times, 2, 31, 44, 55, 167, 223, 251
Newmark, Craig, 21
Newsletter, brand building and, 83
Newspaper, self-syndicated columns, 82
Newsweek, 251
Newteevee.com, 187
Nielson ratings, 159
Nike, 66
Nintendo 64, 169
NPD Market Research Group, 236
Nunes, Julia, 11, 166–167
NyQuil, 238

O'Brien, Conan, 17
O'Connor, Sean, 261
Obama, Barack, 226, 227
Obama, Michelle, 236
ObamaCondoms.com, 229
Ohare, Vinny, 58
Olanoff, Drew, 163
The One Minute Millionaire, 271
OnlineVideoToolkit.com, 177, 189
Oprah, 71, 198, 225
Orman, Suzi, 78
Oxygen bars, 243

Packages, offering, 104–105
Page, Elisa Camahort, 20
Pain, sales and alleviating, 93–97
Palin, Sarah, 227
Palm Pre, 58
Parent-Teacher Association (PTA), 146
Paul Harvey News, 44
Pauling, Linus, 60
PayPal, lack of simplicity, 104, 105
People Magazine, 263
Pepsi, 150, 153
The Perfection of Marketing, 86
PersonalBrandingBlog.com, 78
Personal Branding Magazine, 78
Personallifemedia.com, 11
Pet Rock, 235
Phantom, 243
Philbin, Regis, 44
Pitches, 33
Playboy, 251
Podcasts, subscribers as revenue, 2
Pogue, David, 31
Polk, Mike, 168–169
Polo, 64
Pomplamoose, 168
Portland Beavers, 68
Post-it notes, 56–57
Press releases, moving beyond, 30–34
Prfessor.com, 127
Problogger.net, 118
Proctor, Bob, 70
Productivity, distractions and, 113
Prpuppettheatre, 178
Publicity, negative, 214–216

Quality, branding and, 84
Question Mark Guy, 75
Quicken Loans, 163
Quinn, Leo J., Jr., 254–256
Quotes, price, lack of simplicity, 104–105
QVC, 234

Radio, features as revenue, 2
Recruitment
  free, 103
Red Bull, 64
Red Cross, 162
Reeve, Christopher, 71
Referrals, 137
Regis Philbin Show, 44
Registerfree.com, 38
Remodeling, 81
Reputation, monitoring your, 77
Research, pitches and, 33
Restaurants, 154, 208
Restaurant Owner, 143
Revenue
  goals, 122–123
  internet, 85–92
    environment and, 98–106
    various definitions, 2, 5
  web, 109–110, 111–116
  See also Sales
Reviews, online video, 190
Riccards, Patrick R., 57
Rice, Tom, 268
Richman, Adam, 209
Risk coverage, opportunities for, 240–241
Rivers, Joan, 198, 263
Robertson, Lloyd, 72
Rolls Royce, 243

Roosevelt, Franklin Delano, 71
Rosenberg, Eva, 73–74, 76
Rousell, Sandra, 58
Rowling, J. K., 71
Rowse, Darren, 11, 118
Russell, Bill, 172–173

Sacramento Kings, 69
Sadler, Jason, 62
Sahara Hotel and Casino, 211
Sakurai, Carmen, 57
Salahi, Tareq and Michaele, 226
The Sales Moment, 86
Sales
  funnel, 94–97, 103
  See also Revenue
Save the Mountain, 248–249
Savetz, Kevin, 245
Savetz Publishings, 245
Schawbel, Dan, 78
Schedules, creating, 113
Schembari, Marian, 157–160
Schlessinger, Dr. Laura, 269–270
Search engine optimization (SEO), 125–126
Search.Twitter.com, 152
SEObook.com, 125
Shankman, Peter, 10, 35
Shareasale.com, 146
Simplicity, 98–101, 104
Simpson, Joe, 71
SKY News, 222
The Slanket, 234
SmallBizTrends, 190
Smart Money, 44
Smith, Joe, 227
Smith, Mari, 11
Snuggie, 234, 238–240

SnuggiePubCrawls.com, 239
SnuggieSightings.com, 239
Social media
   branding and, 13–17, 79–80
   to create attention, 148–150
   evolution of, 79
   fund-raising, 162–164
   revenue and, 151–156
Solutions, offering customers,
   93–97
Sony, 168
The Sopranos, 236
Southall, Ben, 260
Spinal muscular atrophy, 34
Spoelstra, Jon, 69
Sports marketers, 67
Squarespace.com, 219
St. Paul Saints, 68
Startup Journal, 55
Sticker Giant, 75
Stocking, Pasha, 223–224
Storytelling, 257–228
   branding and, 84
Strength Coach, 143
Stride gum, 169
Stucker, Cathy, 55
Subscriptions, 2, 136–137
Success Magazine, 273
Sullivan, Andrew "Sully," 139
Super Bowl, 150, 212
Susan G. Komen for the Cure,
   163

Take Me to the River, 236
Talayna's, 210
Tampa Bay Devil Rays, 69
Tax Mama, 73–74, 76
Tax service, 66

Taylor, Dave, 79, 80, 218
Team, using online videos to
   introduce, 191
TechCrunch, 205
Tech Czar, 75
Telemedia Communications,
   70–71
Television
   branding and, 17
   features as revenue, 2
   reality, 233
   See also specific type
Temple, Michael, 57
Templeton, Bob, 71
TenGoldenRules.com, 138
Testimonials, 237–241
   online video, 191
Tew, Alex, 63
TextPad, 58
This Is True, 251, 252
Titanic, 36
Today Show, 34, 169, 185, 198, 205
The Tonight Show with Jay Leno, 44,
   45, 185
"The Top Ten Tricks to Doing
   Your Taxes," 170
Toys for Tots, 23
Trackur.com, 77
Trademark Electronic Search
   System (TESS), 230
Trademark, branding and, 76–77
Traffic Geyser, 193
Training sessions, 132
Trump, Donald, 78
Tubemogul, 192–193
Tweetdeck application, 152
Tweetforals.com, 163
Twestival, 164

Twitter
  branding and, 15, 19
  customer service, 152
  Festival, 164
  followers as revenue, 2
  image and, 218
  social and financial equity, 14

U.S. Government Trademark
    Electronic Search System
    (TESS), 77
UFood Grill, 212
Uniform Resource Locator (URL),
    171
Unique value proposition (UVP),
    85–91, 101, 172
United Way, 162
Universal, 168
University of Akron, 72
USA Today, 34, 44, 223, 239
User generated content (UGC)
    videos, 186

Van Beethoven, Ludwig, 71
Van Duinen, Sharon, 211
Van Stolk, Peter, 22
Vaynerchuk, Gary, 10, 13–14, 17
Veeck, Mike, 67
Venture Beat, 205
Veterinary Insider, 143
Video
  blogs, 154
  as a business strategy, 46–48
  distribution, 192–193
  online, fear of, 176–178
  revenue and, 165–175
  tips and ideas for, 188–191
  viral, 180–187

Vimeo.com, 192–193
Virgin America, 20
Voice, having a, 220–224

Walker, Amy, 169
Wall, Aaron, 125–126
WALL-E, 236
Wall Street Journal, 2, 44, 55
Ward, Missy, 10, 12, 118, 163
Warner, 168
Washington Post, 205, 245
Water, bottled, 243
Weber, Evan, 57
Webinars, free services via,
    103
Weezer, 239
Wells, Jane, 178
Wendy's, 62
Wheeler, Mike, 239–240
Where in the Hell is Matt,
    169
Whiteboards, online videos and,
    190–191
Whole Foods Market, 153
Wiliams, Cory, 168
William, Pete, 271
Willitblend.com, 153, 180–186
Wilson, Joe, 227–228
Winelibrary TV, 17
Wired, 205
Wishlist.com, 144
Woman's Day, 55
Woods, Tiger, 214
Wordtracker.com, 127
Worldofkitsch.com, 235
Wright, George, 180–186

Xbox LIVE, 128

Yahoo!, 230
Yankee Stadium, 271
Yates, Simon, 71
Yoga Universe, 143
Yola.com, 219
You Were Born Rich, 70
YouTube, 2, 11

Partner Program,
  168–173
See also Video, online

Zamost, Aaron, 167
Zappos, 18, 128, 186–187
  Insights, 128, 143